WOMEN, FEMINIST IDENTITY AND SOCIETY IN THE 1980's

CRITICAL THEORY
Interdisciplinary Approaches to
Language, Discourse and Ideology

Series Editors
Iris M. Zavala
Myriam Díaz-Diocaretz

Advisory Editorial Board:

Fernando Lázaro Carreter *(Real Academia Española)*
Jonathan Culler *(Cornell University, Ithaca)*
Teun A. van Dijk *(University of Amsterdam, Amsterdam)*
Roger Fowler *(University of East Anglia, Norwich)*
Claudio Guillén *(Harvard University)*
Fredric Jameson *(University of California, Santa Cruz)*
Cheris Kramarae *(University of Illinois at Urbana-Champaign)*
Teresa de Lauretis *(University of Wisconsin-Milwaukee)*
Cesare Segre *(Università di Pavia)*
Harly Sonne *(Rijksuniversiteit Utrecht, Utrecht)*
Gayatri Ch. Spivak *(Emory University, Atlanta)*

Volume 1

Myriam Díaz-Diocaretz and Iris M. Zavala (eds.)

WOMEN, FEMINIST IDENTITY AND SOCIETY IN THE 1980's
Selected Papers

WOMEN, FEMINIST IDENTITY AND SOCIETY IN THE 1980's
SELECTED PAPERS

edited by

MYRIAM DÍAZ-DIOCARETZ and IRIS M. ZAVALA

JOHN BENJAMINS PUBLISHING COMPANY
AMSTERDAM/PHILADELPHIA

1985

Library of Congress Cataloging in Publication Data

Main entry under title:

Women, feminist identity, and society in the 1980's.

(Critical theory: interdisciplinary approaches to language, discourse, and ideology; v. 1)
    Papers presented at the Utrecht Summer School of Critical Semiotics, held May 31-June 2, 1984.
1. Women's studies -- Congresses. 2. Feminism -- Congresses. 3. Women -- Social conditions -- Congresses. 4. Semiotics and literature -- Congresses. I. Díaz-Diocaretz, Myriam. II. Zavala, Iris M. III. Utrecht Summer School of Critical Semiotics (1st: 1984)
HQ1180.W66   1985   305.4'2   84-28286
ISBN 0-915027-50-X (U.S. hb.)
ISBN 0-915027-51-8 (U.S. pb.)
ISBN 90-272-2401-3 (European hb.)
ISBN 90-272-2402-1 (European pb.)

© Copyright 1985 - All rights reserved.
No part of this book may be reproduced in any form, by print, photoprint, microfilm, or any other means, without written permission from the publisher.

CONTENTS

Foreword   1
Iris M. Zavala

KEYNOTE ADDRESS   5

Notes Toward a Politics of Location   7
Adrienne Rich

SEMIOTIC THEORY: Sexuality, Literature and Culture   23

Female Desire and Sexual Identity   25
Rosalind Coward

Black North-American Women Poets in the Semiotics of Culture   37
Myriam Díaz-Diocaretz

PRACTICAL CRITICISM: Law, Racism and Art   61

Women's Rights as Human Rights: Latin American Countries and
the Organization of American States (OAS)   63
Cecilia Medina

Racism in Everyday Experiences of Black Women   81
Philomena Essed

"I found God in Myself and I loved Her/I loved Her fiercely":
More Thoughts on the Work of Black Women Artists.   101
Michelle Cliff

CONCLUDING REMARKS   127
Iris M. Zavala

CONTRIBUTORS NOTES   137

FOREWORD

The sense that there is a need to liberate women's discourse is reflected in the continuing problems the essays in this volume discuss. They are all lectures given during the first session of the UTRECHT SUMMER SCHOOL OF CRITICAL SEMIOTICS, where, for three days women from the Old and the New World (Holland, England, France, Italy, Scandinavia, India, North America, Latin America, Canada, Curaçao, Surinam, Africa), dialogued on ideology, sex, history, class, social change. Now the dialogue has moved on to the stage of publication of the present volume.

The principal idea of this volume of the Utrecht Summer School of Critical Semiotics, devoted this year to *Women, Feminist Identity and Society in the 1980's*, is to try to surpass the limits between an entirely abstract formal approach to women studies and an equally abstract de-contextualized approach. The general objective is to present and discuss different modes of existence of women's texts and feminist identity in political and poetic discourse on the one hand, and to analyse the factors which determine differing relationships between women and society, and which result in specific forms of identity on the other. Equally important are the cultural mechanisms of production influencing the circulation of women's texts.

Form and content are one, once we understand that discourse (in the widest possible sense of the term) is a social and political phenomenon — social throughout its entire range and in each and every of its factors. Our emphasis on feminist critical stand is aimed at raising issues that extend beyond the texts; they reflect the political concerns that motivated them. No single ideology is a unifying element, but different as the methodology and topics seem to be, there is a profound unity of objectives. There are diverse methods and assumptions used to reach a specific goal; to unveil sexism, ethnocentricity and racism in some of its crudest manifestations. Thus we have divided the volume into three distinct parts: it opens with a keynote address by poet Adrienne Rich, and is followed by two theoretical papers on language and literature, finally three working papers on institutions and the visual arts. Deciphering the interplay of female identity requires a variety of critical approaches: political, legal, sociological, philosophical, linguistic, visual arts and literary. Some important lines of inquiry are sure to arise within this large framework of semiotics of culture.

Adrienne Rich, Philomena Essed and Cecilia Medina, from different perspectives, argue on the importance of "location" (to use Rich's pertinent concept): how race, class, ethnicity and geography shape women's identity, perspectives, points of view, social patterns. Rich's essay constitutes a challenge to some Western European centered feminist assumptions; her radical questioning as to who is *we* raises important social and political implications. Essed and Medina present two very defined groups: Blacks in the Netherlands and Latin American Women respectively. From different view points — Essed's sociological/political, Medina's legal — both show how social institutions circumscribe action, and point to the inroads racism and sexism have made into the support of exploitations and repression. Essed analyzes the systematic manifestations in everyday life in Holland, from the point of view of those who suffer racism.

Myriam Díaz-Diocaretz and Michelle Cliff analyze Black American women's texts, literary and visual, in a complementary way. Within a theoretical framework of semiotics of culture, Díaz-Diocaretz shows how the yearning for a connection which was brutally severed by the double forces of sexism and racism, forged some specific artistic strategies and devices based on the memory factor. As minorities within minorities, Black American poets have created a distinct set of cultural and aesthetic values, based on the rehabilitation of their identity, which the larger culture systematically denigrated. Cliff's incursion into Afro-American visual arts as a re-connection with Africa is bound to stimulate more research in this field. Images, symbols, materials used, form, color, aesthetic standards of Afro-American women artists, are part of a tradition which the slaves were brutally denied.

Rosalind Coward, from a theoretical perspective, centers her attention on the role sexuality plays on current and past issues — philosophy, pornography, media, advertisement. How women's and men's erotic natures differ, and how sexual issues have been used to tighten the grip of social constraints. Philosophical discourse, desire and mass media produced eroticism, are used as tools to reveal some aspects of the sexual roles and fantasies attributed to women (on these particular issues see Snitow, Stansell, Thompson 1983).

The six contributions thus address themselves to a distinct set of women's cultural, political and aesthetic values. Within this perspective of semiotic study of strict nexus between theory and practice, there is a re-location of the very relationship of language to the object and to the speaker. Transmission of information is always simultaneously an appropriation or assimilation of it.

Ideology is semiotic in the sense that it involves the concrete exchange of signs in society and in history. Every word or discourse betrays the ideology of the speaker and is interpreted according to that of the addressee, which may vary according to cultural, historical, geographical and social situations. And, *ça va sans dire* that there is a relationship between sexuality and social formations. Within this overall framework of signs and ideology and theory of communication, we present some crucial problems about women. We take into account the role of the speaking subject not only as a sender of messages, but as a concrete historical, biological, psychic subject. Female experience as it manifests itself through sign-functions, producing sign-functions, criticising other sign-functions. The essays in this volume infer concrete social constraints, family structures, modes of production, political systems all of which shape and structure the activity of thought, as well as the dominant literary modes, and the nature of domination.

The project of critical semiotic theory within this framework, is to map how the physical properties of human beings and of the natural world (voice, energy, body, race, to mention just a few), are socially assumed as signs, as vehicles for social meaning; and how these sign-vehicles are culturally organized into sign systems subject to historical modes of sign production. Women are still regarded as "invisible signs of visibility"; seen as commodities, as signs produced in social discourse by and for men, and excluded from the universe of cultural production and discourse itself (Gayle 1975; Cow 1978, Reuter 1978). Semiotics, then, if it claims to be a critical discipline, can be used to demystify semiotic practice (de Lauretis 1978/79).

I will not describe further the importance of these issues and the questions raised by these essays. Let it suffice to say that *Women, Feminist Identity and Society in the 1980's* explores language, gender, philosophy, women's identity as Blacks, Third World, as well as the nature of domination, feminist criticism and female creativity. We do not pretend to completeness or precision. Only the further development of critical study on feminist identity and society can determine whether the approach taken in the present volume will prove fundamental and productive.

Iris M. Zavala
UTRECHT

Acknowledgments

We are grateful to Claire and John Benjamins and the staff of John Benjamins Publisher, particularly to Anne Porcelijn, for their help and support in preparing this volume. We are also grateful to the collaborators who patiently endured the months of uncertainty; no amount of thanks could indicate our gratitude for their support. Finally, our appreciation to all those colleagues and friends who collaborated with us to organize this conference at the University of Utrecht.

REFERENCES

Cow, Elizabeth 1978. "Women as Signs." *M/F*: 49-63.
Lauretis, Teresa de. 1978/79. "Semiotics. Theory and Social Practice. A Critical History of Italian Semiotics." *Diacritics*: 1-14.
Rubin, Gayle. 1975. "The Traffic in Women. Notes on the Political Economy of Sex". In Rayna R. Reiter, ed. *Toward and Anthropology of Women*. New York: Monthly Review Press: 157-210.
Snitow, Ann; Christine Stansell, Sharon Thompson, eds. 1983. *Powers of Desire. The Politics of Sexuality*. New York: Monthly Review Press.

ered an issue editing
KEYNOTE ADDRESS

NOTES TOWARD A POLITICS OF LOCATION

Talk for Conference on Women, Feminist Identity and
Society in the 1980's, Utrecht,
Holland, June 1 1984

Adrienne Rich

I am to speak these words in Europe, but I have been searching for them in the United States of America. A few years ago I would have spoken of the common oppression of women, the gathering movement of women around the globe, the hidden history of women's resistance and bonding, the failure of all previous politics to recognize the universal shadow of patriarchy, the belief that women, now, in a time of rising consciousness and global emergency may join across all national and cultural boundaries to create a society free of domination, in which "sexuality, politics, ... work .... intimacy .... thinking itself will be transformed."(Rich 1976: 286)

I would have spoken these words as a feminist who "happened" to be a white United States citizen, conscious of my government's proven capacity for violence and arrogance of power, but as self-separated from that government, quoting without second thoughts Virginia Woolf's statement in *Three Guineas* that "As a woman I have no country. As a woman I want no country. As a woman my country is the whole world."

This is not what I come here to say in 1984. I come here with notes, but without absolute conclusions. This is not a sign of loss of faith or hope. These notes are the marks of a struggle to keep moving, a struggle for accountability.

Beginning to write, then getting up. Stopped by the movements of a huge early bumble bee which has somehow gotten inside this house and is reeling, bumping, stunning itself against windowpanes and sills. I open the front door and speak to it, trying to attract it outside. It is looking for what it needs, just as I am, and like me, it has gotten trapped in a place where it cannot fulfill its own life. I could open the jar of honey on the kitchen counter and perhaps it would take honey from that jar; but its life-process, its work, its mode of being, cannot be fulfilled inside this house.

And I, too, have been bumping my way against glassy panes, falling half-stunned, gathering myself up and crawling, then again taking-off, searching.

I don't hear the bumblebee any more, and I leave the front door. I sit down and pick up a second-hand, faintly-annotated student copy of Marx's *The German Ideology*, which "happens" to be lying on the table.

I will speak these words in Europe but I am having to search for them in the United States of North America. When I was ten or eleven, early in World War II, a girl-friend and I used to write each other letters which we addressed like this:

> Adrienne Rich
> 14 Edgevale Road
> Baltimore, Maryland
> The United States of America
> The Continent of North America
> The Western Hemisphere
> The Earth
> The Solar System
> The Universe

You could see your own house as a tiny fleck on an ever-widening landscape; or as the center of it all, from which the circles expanded into the infinite unknown.

It is that question of feeling at the center that gnaws at me now — at the center of what?

As a woman I have a country; as a woman I cannot divest myself of that country merely by condemning its government, or by saying three times, "As a woman my country is the whole world." Tribal loyalties aside, and even if nation-states are now just pretexts used by multinational conglomerates to serve their interest, I need to understand how a place on the map is also a place in history, within which as a woman, a Jew, a lesbian, a feminist, I am created and trying to create.

Begin, though, not with a continent or a country or a house, but with the geography closest-in. The body. Here at least I know I exist, that living human individual whom the young Marx called "the first premise of all human history". But it was not as a Marxist that I turned to this place, back from philosophy and literature and science and theology in which I had looked for myself in vain. It was as a radical feminist.

The politics of pregnability and motherhood. The politics of orgasm. The politics of rape and incest, of abortion, birth control, forcible sterilization. Of prostitution and marital sex. Of what had been named sexual liberation. Of prescriptive heterosexuality. Of lesbian existence.

And Marxist feminists were often pioneers in this work. But for many women I knew, the need to begin with the female body — our own — was understood not as applying a Marxist principle *to* women but as locating the grounds from which to speak with authority *as* women. Not to transcend this body but to reclaim it. To re-connect our thinking and speaking with the body of this particular living human individual, a woman. Begin, we said, with the material, with matter, mma, madre, mutter, moeder, modder, etc. etc.

Begin with the material. Pick up again the long struggle against lofty and privileged abstraction. Perhaps this is the core of revolutionary process, whether it calls itself Marxist or Third World or feminist or all three. Long before the 19th century, the empirical witch of the European Middle Ages trusting her senses, practising her tried remedies against the anti-material, anti-sensuous, anti-empirical dogmas of the Church. Dying for that, by the millions. "A female-led peasant rebellion"? in any event, a rebellion against the idolatry of pure ideas, the belief that ideas have a life of their own and float along above the heads of ordinary people — women, the poor, the uninitiated (Ehrenreich & English, 1973).

Abstractions severed from the doings of living people, fed back to people as slogans.

Theory — the seeing of patterns, showing the forest as well as the trees — theory can be a dew that rises from the earth and collects in the raincloud and returns to earth, over and over. But if it doesn't smell of the earth, it isn't good for the earth.

I wrote a sentence just now and x'd it out. In it I said that women have always understood the struggle against free-floating abstraction even when we were intimidated by abstract ideas. I don't want to write that kind of sentence now, the sentence that begins, "Women have always...." We started by rejecting the sentences that began, "Women have always had an instinct for mothering" or, "Women have always been in subjugation to men." If we have learned anything, in these years of late twentieth century feminism, it's that that "always" blots out what we really need to know: when, where and under what conditions has the statement been true?

The absolute necessity to raise these questions in the world: where, when, and under what conditions have women acted and been acted-on, as women? Wherever people are struggling against subjection, the specific subjection of women, through our location in a female body, from now on has to be addressed. The necessity to go on speaking of it, refusing to let the discussion go on as before, speaking where silence has been advised and enforced, not just about our subjection but about our active presence and practise as women. We believed (I go on believing) that the liberation of women is a wedge driven into all other radical thought, can open out the structures of resistance, unbind the imagination, connect what's been dangerously disconnected. Let us pay attention now, we said, to women: let men and women make a conscious act of attention when women speak, let us insist on kinds of process which allow more women to speak, let us get back to earth. Not as paradigm for "woman", but as place of location.

Perhaps we need a moratorium on saying "the body". For it's also possible to abstract the body. When I write "the body" I see nothing in particular. To write "my body" plunges me into lived experience, particularity: I see scars, disfigurements, discolorations, damages, losses, as well as what pleases me. White skin, marked and scarred by three pregnancies, a sterilization, progressive arthritis, four joint operations, calcium deposits, no rapes, no abortions, much time at the typewriter, and so forth. To say "the body" lifts me away from what has given me a primary perspective. To say "my body" reduces the temptation to grandiose assertions.

This body. White, female; or, female, white. The first obvious, lifelong facts. But I was born in the white section of a hospital which separated Black and white women in labor and Black and white babies in the nursery, just as it separated Black and white bodies in its morgue. I was defined as white before I was defined as female.

The politics of location. Even to begin with my body I have to say that from the outset that body had more than one identity. When I was carried out of the hospital into the world, I was viewed and treated as female, but also viewed and treated as white — by both Black and white people. I was located by color and sex as surely as a Black child was located by color and sex — though the implications of white identity were mystified by the presumption that white people are the center of the universe.

To locate myself in my body means more than understanding what it has meant to me to have a vulva and clitoris and uterus and breasts. It means recognizing this white skin, the places it has taken me, the places it has not let me go.

Trying as women to see from the center. "A politics", I wrote once, "of asking women's questions." (Rich 1979). We are not "the woman question" asked by somebody else, we are the women who ask the questions.

Trying to see so much, aware of so much to be seen, brought into the light, changed. Breaking down again and again the false male universal. Piling piece by piece of concrete experience side by side, comparing, beginning to discern patterns. Anger, frustration with Marxist or Leftist dismissals of these questions, this struggle. Easy now to call this disillusionment facile, but the anger was deep, the frustration real, both in personal relationships and political organizations. I wrote in 1975: *Much of what is narrowly termed "politics" seems to rest on a longing for certainty even at the cost of honesty, for an analysis which, once given, need not be re-examined. Such is the dead-endedness — for women — of Marxism in our time.* (Rich 1979: 193)

And it has felt like a dead-end wherever politics has been externalized, cut off from the on-going lives of women or of men, rarefied into an élite jargon, defined by little sects who feed off each others' errors.

But even as we shrugged away Marx along with the academic Marxists and the sectarian Left, some of us, calling ourselves radical feminist, never meant anything less by women's liberation than the creation of a society without domination; we never meant less than the making-new of all relationships. The problem was that we did not know who we meant when we said "we".

The literature of the West (I read) is the white man's reflection of himself. So should it be supplemented by the white woman's reflection of herself? And nothing more?

This from the East German novelist Christa Wolf, in her recent book, *Cassandra*. (Wolf 1984: 220)

.....the power men everywhere wield over women, power which has become a model for every other form of exploitation and illegitimate control. (Rich 1981) I wrote these words in 1977 at the end of an essay called "Compulsory Heterosexuality and Lesbian Existence". Patriarchy as the "model" for other forms of domination — this idea was not original with me, it has been put forward insistently by white Western feminists, and in 1972 I had quoted from Lévi-Strauss: *I would go so far as to say that even before slavery or class domination existed, men built an approach to women that would serve one day to introduce differences among us all.* (Rich 1979: 84)

Living for fifty-some years, having watched even minor bits of history unfold, I am less quick than I once was to search for single "causes" or origins in the dealings among human beings. But suppose that we could trace back and establish that patriarchy has been everywhere the model — to what choices of action does that lead us in the present? Patriarchy exists nowhere in a pure state; we are the latest to set foot in a tangle of oppressions grown up and around each other for centuries. This isn't the old children's game where you choose one strand of color in the web and follow it back to find your prize, ignoring the others as mere distractions. The prize is life itself, and most women in the world must fight for our lives on many fronts at once.

We....often find it difficult to separate race from class from sex oppression because in our lives they are most often experienced simultaneously. We know that there is such a thing as racial-sexual oppression which is neither solely racial nor solely sexual.....We need to articulate the real class situation of persons who are not merely raceless, sexless workers but for whom racial and sexual oppression are significant determinants in their working/economic lives.

This from the 1977 Combahee River Collective Statement, a major document of the U.S. women's movement, which gives a clear and uncompromising Black feminist naming to the experience of *simultaneity of oppressions*.[1] (Smith, ed. 1984)

Even in the struggle against free-floating abstraction, we have abstracted. Marxists and radical feminists have both done this, why not admit it, get it said, so we can get on to the work to be done, back down to earth again? The faceless, sexless, raceless proletariat. The faceless, raceless, classless category of "all women". Both creations of white western self-centeredness.

To come to terms with the circumscribing nature of (our) whiteness. (Joseph 1981) Marginalized though we have been as women, as white and western makers of theory, we also marginalize others. Because our lived experience is thoughtlessly white, because even our "women's cultures" are rooted in some western tradition. Recognizing our location, having to name the ground we're coming from, the conditions we have taken for granted — there is a confusion between our claims to the white and western eye and the woman-seeing eye, (Frye 1983: 171) fear of losing the centrality of the one even as we claim the other.

How does the white western feminist define theory? Is it something made only by white women, and only by women acknowledged as writers? How does the white western feminist define "an idea"? Who are the "women of ideas"? How do we actively work to build a white western feminist consciousness that is not simply centered on itself, that resists white circumscribing?

It was in the writings but also the actions and speeches and sermons of Black United States citizens that I began to experience the meaning of my whiteness as a point of location for which I needed to take responsibility. It was in reading poems by contemporary Cuban women that I began to experience the meaning of North America as a location which had also shaped my ways of seeing and my ideas of who and what was important, a location for which I was also responsible. I travelled then to Nicaragua, where, in a tiny, richly green yet impoverished country, in a four-year-old society dedicated to eradicating poverty, under the hills of the Nicaragua-Honduras border, I could physically feel the weight of the United States of North America, its military forces, its vast appropriations of money, its mass media, at my back; I could feel what it means, dissident or not, to be part of that raised boot of power, the cold shadow we cast everywhere to the south.

I come from a country stuck fast for forty years in the deepfreeze of history. Any United States citizen alive today has been saturated with Cold War rhetoric, the horrors of communism, the betrayals of socialism, the warning that any collective restructuring of society spells the end of personal freedom. And yes, there have been horrors and betrayals, deserving open discussion. But we are not invited to consider the butcheries of Stalinism alongside the butcheries of white supremacism and Manifest Destiny. We are not urged to help create a more liveable society in response to the one we are taught to dread. Discourse itself is frozen at this level. Tonight as I turned a switch searching for "the news", that shinily animated silicone mask was on television again, telling the citizens of my country we are menaced by Communism from El Salvador, that Communism — Soviet-variety, obviously — is on the move in Central America, that freedom is imperilled, that the suffering peasants of Latin America must be stopped just as Hitler had to be stopped.

The discourse has never really changed; it is wearyingly abstract. (Lillian Smith, white anti-racist writer and activist, spoke of the "deadly sameness" of abstraction.) It allows no differences among places, times, cultures, conditions, movements. Words which should possess a depth and breadth of allusions, words like socialism, communism, democracy, collectivism — are stripped of their historical roots. The many faces of the struggles for social justice and independence, reduced to an ambition to dominate the world.

Is there a connection between this state of mind — the Cold War mentality, the attribution of all our problems to an external enemy — and a form of feminism so focussed on male evil and female victimization that it, too, allows for no differences among women, men, places, times, cultures, conditions, movements? Living in the climate of an enormous either/or, we absorb some of it, unless we actively take heed.

In the United States large numbers of people have been cut off from their own process and movement. We have been hearing for forty years that we are the guardians of freedom, while "behind the Iron Curtain" all is duplicity and manipulation, if not sheer terror. Yet the legacy of fear lingering after the witch-hunts of the fifties hangs on like the after-smell of a burning. The sense of obliquity, mystery, paranoia, surrounding the American Communist Party after the Krushchev Report of 1956: the Party lost 30.000 members within weeks, and few who remained were talking about it. To be a Jew, a homosexual, any kind of marginal person, was to be liable for suspicion of being "Communist". A blanketing snow had begun to drift over the radical history of the United States.

And — though parts of the North American feminist movement actually sprang from the Black movements of the Sixties and the student anti-war movement — feminists have suffered not only from the burying and distortion of women's experience, but from the overall burying and distortion of the great movements for social change. (Bulkin 1984)

The first American woman astronaut is interviewed by the liberal-feminist editor of a mass-circulation women's magazine. She is a splendid creature, healthy, young, thick dark head of hair, scientific doctorates from an elite university, an athletic self-confidence. She is also white. She speaks of the future of space, the potential uses of spaces colonies by private industry, especially for producing materials which can be advantageously processed under conditions of weightlessness. Pharmaceuticals, for example. By extension one thinks of chemicals. Neither of these two spirited women speak of the alliances between the the military and the "private" sector of the North American economy. nor do they speak of Depo-Provera, Valium, Librium, napalm, dioxin. *When big companies decide that it's now to their advantage to put a lot of their money into production of materials in space....we'll really get the funding that we need*, says the astronaut. No mention of who "we" are, and what "we" need funding for; no questions about the poisoning and impoverishment of women here on earth, or of the earth itself. Women too may leave the earth behind.(*MS* January 1984: 86)

The astronaut is young, feels her own power, works hard for her exhilaration. She has swung out over the earth and come back, one more time passed all the tests. It's not that I expect her to come back to earth as Cassandra. But this experience of hers has nothing to do with the liberation of women. A female proletariat — uneducated, ill-nourished, unorganized, and largely from the Third World — will create the profits which will stimulate the "big companies" to invest in space.

On a split screen in my brain I see two versions of her story: the backward gaze through streaming weightlessness to the familiar globe, pale blue and green and white, the strict and sober presence of it, the true intuition of relativity battering the heart; and the swiftly calculated move to a further suburb, the male technocrats and the women they have picked and tested, leaving the familiar globe behind: the toxic rivers, the cancerous wells, the strangled valleys, the closed-down urban hospitals, the shattered schools, the atomic desert blooming, the lilac suckers run wild, the blue grape-hyacinths spreading, the ailanthus and kudzu doing their final desperate part: the beauty that won't travel, that can't be stolen away.

A movement for change lives in feelings, actions, and words. Whatever circumscribes or mutilates our feelings makes it more difficult to act: abstract thinking, tribal loyalties, every kind of self-righteousness, the arrogance of believing ourselves at the center. It's hard to look back on the limits of my understanding a year, five years ago — how did I look without seeing, hear without listening? It's difficult to be generous to earlier selves, and keeping faith with the continuity of our journeys is especially hard in the United States, where identities and loyalties have been shed and replaced without a tremor, all in the name of becoming "American". Yet how, except through ourselves, do we discover what moves other people to change? Our old fears and denials — what helps us let go of them? What makes us decide we have to re-educate ourselves, even those of us with "good" educations? A politicized life ought to sharpen both the senses and the memory.

The difficulty of saying I — another phrase from Christa Wolf. (Wolf 1970: 174) But once having said it, as we realize the necessity to go further, isn't there a difficulty of saying "we"? *You cannot speak for me. I cannot speak for us.* Two thoughts: there is no liberation that only knows how to say "I". There is no collective movement that speaks for each of us all the way through.

And so even ordinary pronouns become a political problem. (Reagon 1983: 356-368 & Bulkin 1984: 103, 190-193)

Sixty-four cruise missiles in Greenham Common and Molesworth.
One hundred and twelve at Comiso.
Ninety-six Pershing II Missiles in West Germany.
Ninety-six for Belgium and the Netherlands.
That is the projection for the next few years.[2]
Thousands of women, in Europe and the United States, saying *no* to this and to the militarization of the world.

.... *An approach which traces militarism back to patriarchy and patriarchy back to the fundamental quality of maleness can be demoralizing and even paralyzing....Perhaps it is possible to be less fixed on the discovery of "original causes". It might be more useful to ask, How do these values and behaviors get repeated generation after generation?* (Enloe 1983: Ch. 8)

The valorization of manliness and masculinity. The armed forces as the extreme embodiment of the patriarchal family. The archaic idea of women as a "home front" even as the missiles are deployed in the backyards of Wyoming and Mutlangen. The growing urgency that an anti-nuclear, anti-militarist movement must be a feminist movement, must be a socialist movement, must be an anti-racist, anti-imperialist movement. That it's not enough to fear for the people we know, our own kind, ourselves. Nor is it empowering to give ourselves up to abstract terrors of pure annihilation. The anti-nuclear, anti-military movement cannot sweep away the missiles as a movement to save white civilization in the West. The movement for change is a changing movement, changing itself, de-masculinizing itself, de-westernizing itself, becoming a critical mass that is saying in so many different voices, languages, gestures, actions: *It must change. We ourselves can change it.*

We — who are not the same. We who are many and do not want to be the same.

Trying to watch myself in the process of writing this, I keep coming back to something Sheila Rowbotham, the British socialist-feminist, wrote in *Beyond the Fragments*:

> ....*there are enormous and serious difficulties in the relationship between groups of people who have been subordinated and theory. A movement helps you to overcome some of the oppressive distancing of theory and this has been a....continuing creative endeavour of women's liberation. But some paths are not mapped and our footholds vanish....I see what I'm writing as part of a wider claiming which is beginning. I am part of the difficulty myself. The difficulty is not out there.* (Rowbotham, Segal & Wainwright 1981: 55-56)

My difficulties too are not out there — except in the social conditions that make all this necessary. I do not any longer *believe*, my feelings do not allow me to believe, that the white eye sees from the center. Yet I often find myself thinking as if I still believed that were true. Or rather, my thinking stands still. I feel in a state of arrest, as if my brain and heart were refusing to speak to each other. My brain, a woman's brain, has exulted in breaking the taboo against women thinking, has taken off on the wind, saying, *I am the woman who asks the questions.* My heart has been learning in a much more humble and laborious way, learning that feelings are useless without facts, that all privilege is ignorant at the core.

The United States has never been a white country, though it has long served what white men defined as their interests. The Mediterranean was never white. England, Northern Europe, if ever absolutely white, are so no longer. In a Leftist bookstore in Manchester, a Third World poster: WE ARE HERE BECAUSE YOU WERE THERE. In Europe there have always been the Jews, the original ghetto dwellers, identified as a racial type, who suffered under pass laws and special entry taxes, enforced relocations, massacres: the scapegoats, the aliens, never seen as truly European but as part of that darker world that must be controlled, eventually exterminated. Today the cities of Europe have new scapegoats as well: the diaspora from the old colonial empires. Is anti-Semitism the model for racism? Or racism for anti-Semitism? Once more, where does the question lead us? Don't we have to start here, where we are, forty years after the Holocaust, in the churn of Middle Eastern violence, on the edge of decisive ferment in South Africa? — not in some debate over origins and precedents but in the recognition of simultaneous oppressions.

I've been thinking a lot about this obsession with origins. It seems a way of stopping time in its tracks. The Neolithic sacred triangles, the Minoan vases with staring eyes and breasts, the female figurines of Anatolia — weren't they concrete evidence of a kind, like Sappho's fragments, for earlier woman-affirming cultures, cultures that enjoyed centuries of peace? But haven't they also served as arresting images, which have kept women attached and immobilized? Human activity didn't stop in Crete or Çatal Hüyuk. We can't build a society free from domination by fixing our sights backward on some long-ago tribe or city.

The continuing spiritual power of an image lives in the interplay between what it reminds us of — what it *brings to mind* — and our own continuing actions in the present. When the labrys becomes a badge for a cult of Minoan goddesses, when the wearer of the labrys has ceased to ask herself what she is doing on this earth, where her love of women is taking her, it too becomes abstraction — lifted away from the heat and friction fo human activity. The Jewish star on my neck must serve me both as reminder and as a goad to continuing, and changing, responsibility.

When I learn that in 1913 mass women's marches were held in South Africa which caused the rescinding of entry permit laws; that in 1956 20,000 women assembled in Pretoria to protest pass laws for women, that resistance to these laws was carried out in remote country villages and punished by shootings, beatings, and burnings; that in 1959 two thousand women demonstrated in Durban against laws which provided beerhalls for African men and criminalized women's traditional home brewing; that at one and the same time African women have played a major role alongside men in resisting apartheid, I have to ask myself why it took me so long to learn these chapters of women's history, why the leadership and strategies of African women have been so unrecognized as theory in action, by white western feminist thought. (And in a book by two men, entitled *South African Politics* and published in 1982, there is one entry under "Women" (franchise) and no reference anywhere to women's political leadership and mass actions.)[3]

When I read that a major strand in the conflicts of the past decade in Lebanon has been political organizing by women of women, across class and tribal and religious lines, women working and teaching together within refugee camps and armed communities, and of the violent undermining of their efforts through the Civil War and the Israeli invasion, I am forced to think. (Wheatley 1984) Iman Khalife, the young teacher who tried to organize a silent peace march on the Christian-Moslem border of Beirut — a protest which was quelled by the threat of a massacre of the participants — Iman Khalife and women like her do not come out of nowhere. But we, Western feminists, living under other kinds of conditions, are not encouraged, to know this background.

And I turn to Etel Adnan's brief extraordinary novel *Sitt Marie Rose*, about a middle-class Christian Lebanese woman tortured for joining the Palestinian Resistance; and read:

> She was also subject to another great delusion believing that women are protected from repression, and that the leaders considered political fights to be strictly between males. In fact, with women's greater access to certain powers, they began to watch them more closely, and perhaps with even greater hostility. Every feminine act, even charitable and seemingly unpolitical ones, were regarded as a rebellion in this world where women had always played servile roles. Marie Rose inspired scorn and hate long before the fateful day of her arrest. (Adnan 1982: 101)

In almost everything I read these days there are women getting up before dawn, in the blackness before the point of light, in the twilight before sunrise, there are women rising earlier than men and children, to break the ice, to start the stove, to put up the pap, the coffee, the rice, to iron the pants, to braid the hair, to pull the day's water up from the well, to boil water for tea, to wash the children for school, to pull the vegetables and start the walk to market, to run to catch the bus for the work that is paid. I don't know when most women sleep. In big cities at dawn women are travelling home after cleaning offices all night, or waxing the halls of hospitals, or sitting up with the old and sick and frightened, at the hour when death is supposed to do its work.

In Peru: "Women invest hours in cleaning tiny stones and chaff out of beans, wheat and rice; they shell peas and clean fish and grind spices in small mortars. They buy bones or tripe at the market and cook cheap, nutritious soups. They repair clothes until they will not sustain another patch. They....search....out the cheapest school uniforms, payable in the greatest number of installments. They trade old magazines for plastic washbasins and buy second-hand toys and shoes. They walk long distances to find a spool of thread at a slightly lower price." (Figueroa & Anderson 1981)

The unpaid female labor which means the survival of the poor.

In minimal light I see her, over and over, her inner clock pushing her out of bed with her heavy and maybe painful limbs, her breath breathing life into her stove, her house, her family, taking the last cold swatch of night on her body, meeting the sudden leap of the rising sun.

In my white North American world they have tried to tell me that this woman — politicized by intersecting forces — doesn't think and reflect on her life. That her ideas are not real ideas like those of Karl Marx and Simone de Beauvoir. That her calculations, her spiritual philosophy, her gifts for law and ethics, her daily emergency political decisions, are merely instinctual or conditioned reactions. That only certain kinds of people can make theory, that white minds are capable of formulating everything, that white feminism can know for "all women", that only when a white mind formulates is the formulation to be taken seriously.

It seems to me that these opinions can only isolate those who hold them, from the great movements for bread and justice within and against which women define ourselves.

Once again: who is *we*?
This is the end of these notes but it is not an ending.

NOTES

1) For a description of simultaneity of African Women's oppression under apartheid see also Hilda Bernstein, *For Their Triumphs and For Their Tears: Women in Apartheid South Africa*. Internaţional Defence and Aid Fund, London 1978.

2) Information as of May 1984 thanks to the War Resisters League.

3) *Women Under Apartheid*, International Defence and Aid Fund for Southern Africa, in cooperation with United Nations Centre against Apartheid. London, 1981, pp. 87-99; and Leonard Thompson and Andrew Prior, *South African Politics*, Yale University Press 1982.

REFERENCES

Adnan, Etel. 1982. *Sitt Marie Rose*. Translated from the French by Georgina Kleege. Post Apollo Press.

Bulkin, Elly. 1984. "Hard Ground: Jewish Identity, Racism and Anti-Semitism" Bulkin, E., M.B. Pratt & B. Smith, *Yours in Struggle: Three Perspectives on Anti-Semitism and Racism*. Brooklyn, N.Y.: Long Haul Press.

Ehrenreich, Barbara and Deidre English. 1973. *Witches, Midwives and Nurses: A History of Women Healers*. Old Westbury, N.Y.: The Feminist Press.

Enloe, Cynthia. 1983. *Does Khaki Become You? The Militarisation of Women's Lives*. London: Pluto Press.

Figueroa, Blanca and Jeanine Anderson. 1981. "Women in Peru". International Reports: Women and Society.

Frye, Marilyn. 1983. *The Politics of Reality*. Trumansburg, N.Y.: Crossing Press.

Joseph, Gloria I. 1981. "The Incompatible Ménage à Trois: Marxism, Feminism and Racism". Lydia Sargent (ed.) *Women and Revolution*. Boston: South End Press.

Lorde, Audre. 1984. *Sister Outsider: Essays and Speeches*. Trumansburg N.Y.: The Crossing Press.

Reagon, Bernice. 1983. "Turning the Century". in Smith.

Rich, Adrienne. 1976. *Of Woman Born*. New York: W.W. Norton Co.

-----. 1979. *On Lies, Secrets and Silence*. New York: W.W. Norton Co.
-----. 1981. "Compulsory Heterosexuality and Lesbian Existence". Published in Dutch ("Gedwongen Heterosexualiteit en Lesbisch Bestaan"), translated by Patty Pattynama. Amsterdam: Lust & Gratie.
Smith, Barbara. (ed.) 1983. *Home Girls: A Black Feminist Anthology*. New York: Kitchen Table Women of Color Press.
Rowbotham, Sheila, Lynne Segal and Hilary Wainwright. 1981. *Beyond The Fragments: Feminism and the Making of Socialism*. Boston: Alyson Publications.
Wheatley, Helen. 1984. "Palestinian Women in Lebanon: Targets of Repression". *TWANAS*, Third World Student Newspaper, University of California, Santa Cruz.
Wolf, Christa. 1970. *The Quest for Christa T*. Translated from the German by Christopher Middleton. New York: Farrar, Straus and Giroux.
-----. 1984. *Cassandra: A Novel and Four Essays*. Translated from the German by Jan van Heurck. New York: Farrar, Straus and Giroux.

SEMIOTIC THEORY: SEXUALITY, LITERATURE AND CULTURE

FEMALE DESIRE AND SEXUAL IDENTITY

Rosalind Coward

Desire, the word, like the experience, tends to run off in all directions. Diffuse, difficult to pin down and give one meaning but it is always assumed to be inordinately important.

In so far as sexuality is discussed and written about, it's the term desire which is currently in the foreground. Not the term desire, derived from Lacanian psychoanalysis, implying a fundamental condition of the human being, separable from need and demand and forever unsatisfiable, but more broadly as a term implying our deepest needs within sexuality. More than sex or lust, definitely separable from love with all its ideological overtones, 'desire' is used to refer to what is most fundamental to our sense of selves in sex, what we really want and what we are driven by.

The *theoretical* investigation of desire has become an issue of some importance within contemporary feminism, but this is somewhat curious because *on the surface* at least, the issues of sex, and of sexual choices no longer appear to be at the forefront of feminist politics. Instead the issue of race and class division is uppermost in women's minds or the question of women's role in the peace movements, or again the apparently more pressing issues of *men's* sexuality and what to do about pornography and sexual violence (particularly urgent in England where new and repressive legislation about video nasties is currently going through parliament).

So why, when there appear to be more immediate problems than the theoretical investigation of sexuality, should many women still pursue an understanding of desire?

The reason, I think, is twofold. Firstly, and this is the position which I advance in my own book, *Female Desire*, (Coward 1984) female desire is crucial to our whole social structure. Our desire as women is one of the primary mechanisms by which consent for a particular way of living is constantly sought and frequently achieved. Secondly, more directly in relation to feminist debates, I believe that even if the issue of sexual identity has gone temporarily underground, assumptions about sexuality still remain crucial to feminism. Indeed, I would go so far as to say that many of the 'more pressing' problems and divisions of current feminist politics are retracing some of the unresolved questions around sexuality. In response many women are still calling for the importance of understanding our desire both personally and politically.

In *Female Desire*, I suggest female — or perhaps I should call it feminine — desire is to some extent the *lynch pin* of a consumerist society. Everywhere women are offered pleasure — pleasure for losing weight, pleasure for preparing beautiful meals, pleasure if we acquire something new — a new body, a new house, a new outfit, a new relationship, a new baby.

Pleasure is western society's permanent special offer for women. But some drive is required to take up that offer. And it is female desire which makes us respond and take up that offer. To be a woman is to be constantly addressed, to be constantly scrutinised, to have our desire constantly courted — in the kitchen, on the streets, in the world of fashion, in films and in fiction. Issuing forth from books and magazines, from films and television, from the radio, there are endless questions about what women desire, endless theories and opinions offered. Desire is stimulated and endlessly defined. Everywhere it seems female desire is sought, bought, packaged and consumed.

Female desire is courted with the promise of future perfection, by the lure of achieving ideals — ideal legs, ideal hair, ideal homes, ideal cream cakes, ideal relationships. Such ideals don't exist in reality, except as the end product of some elaborate photographic techniques or the work of complicated fantasies. But these ideals are held out to women everywhere, all the time. Things may be bad, life may be difficult, relationships may be unsatisfying, you may be feeling undervalued or unfulfilled at work, but there's always the promise of improvement. If only you could achieve these personal improvements, everything could be transformed, you'll almost certainly feel better. Its not the social structure or men that are seen as the problem but your own failure to come up to scratch. Female dissatisfaction is constantly recast in the discourses surrounding and dominating us, as desire. Constantly we are made to feel desire for something more, for a perfect reworking of what has gone before — dissatisfaction is displaced into desire for an ideal.

In *Female Desire*, I attempt a sort of semiotics of this desire, tracing the lure of pleasure that is regularly (but differently) held out to women in different discourses. I look at food photography, at family snapshots, at the imagery of the ideal home, and I look at the fantasies of female desire in the various fictional forms which we consume — in romantic fiction, in what

I call women's novels, and in England's longest running soap opera, the Royal Family. I look at the definitions of desire which are constantly mobilised and held our for women in popular music, on problem pages and in the dominant discourses with which we talk about sex. Again and again, we come across the mobilisation of female desire by the constructions of ideal moments, nowhere so true as in the way photographic and filmic imagery has been directed into women's lives.

Take the issue of food photography, the pictures of sumptious food and elaborate recipes with which women are regularly bombarded. Innocent enough, surely? But I argue these pictures stimulate a desire, which reinforces women's position of subordination.

In many ways these pictures directed at women can be compared with pornography. This is food pornography. Like sexual porn., food pornography is a sex-specific mobilising of desire or appetite which tends to leave the opposite sex stone cold. Like sexual porn, there's a hard-core and soft core to food pornography. Sexual porn has the supposedly illicit hard-core, and a soft core version widely available in the daily newspapers and in the everyday representations of women in film. In food porn, there are the pictures aimed at slimmers, the forbidden fruits, the cream cakes and pancakes on which slimmers can feast their eyes only. Then there's the soft-core, the widely available images dominating women's magazines, recipe books and billboards.

These sex-specific representations re-inforce the position of the sexes. Just as sexual porn directed at men feeds off women's subordination by representing women as endlessly desiring and available for men's pressing sexual needs, so food pictures give messages to women about their place in society. The primary message of these appetising photos is that oral appetites are permissable for women. We don't as women have any representations which so blatantly encourage our sexual appetites, but around food we are presumed to be ever hungry voracious feeders. Sexual porn teaches that men's genital urges are perfectly alright and shoud be instantly satisfied. Food pornography seems to tell women that oral appetites are O.K.

But of course it is not as simple as that. As in so many things for women, we are being encouraged in a desire which can't be satisfied unproblematically. Food is, after all, going to make us fat, and getting fat runs counter to the prevailing ideology about women's shape. We are tantalised with pictures of food but we daren't indulge in case we overspill the limits set for our body by the prevailing ideal — the fatless, firm, lean body much advertised by the likes of Jane Fonda. This ideal is of an almost adolescent body, and represents a disgust with mature flesh, a disgust with the idea of fat, as if it was some kind of advertisement for your lack of self-control, your greedy indulgence of the pleasures of appetite. So women's appetite and desire for food is stimulated so long as we don't really indulge it. And this is the other aspect of food pornography. It teaches us to pursue an interest in oral pleasures so long as they are directed primarily to the servicing of others, that is, usually men. For food is photographed in a very particular way; its a regime of ideal imagery, the culinary equivalent of the removal of unsightly hairs on glamour models. The photographs, like those of models, are idealised, touched up, represent food at a perfect moment. And, what's more, any evidence of the labour women do to prepare food is totally suppressed. These pictures never show chaotic and steamy kitchens, the inevitable mess which cooking involves. They only ever show some imaginary perfect moment, the end-product of the labour when woman, the perfect hostess, lays her gift on the table for others to enjoy.

What is problematic about this is that women get trapped in a desire for perfection which is all about servicing others *and* about downgrading the value of women's labour. We are lured into a desire for preparing lovely food while hiding and devaluing the labour which women's domestic work inevitably involves.

The example may seem slight, but the point of this analysis is to show how even at the most everyday level, even in the most mundane moments of our existence, female desire is stimulated, mobilised, and tied to structures which ultimately oppress us. Here we are lured by pleasure but its a pleasure which even if fulfilled can never bring us satisfaction as women, for we will be caught in those constructions of woman which work against us.

In the analysis of *Female Desire*, I realised that it was important not to treat these practices of representation or discourses as something coming from outside women, as it were, and imposing false and limiting stereotypes. The problem is deeper than that. Instead it seemed crucial to understand the desire presumed by various discourses, to understand the work undertaken around women to construct a constant lure of pleasure, a promise of satisfaction. The more I looked the more I became convinced that there was no one universal and timeless female desire arising from our feminine construction. Instead desire in discourses and representations was multiple and plural. And more important it is the representations and discourses around female pleasure themselves which were producing and sustaining feminine positions. Feminine positions are produced as responses to pleasures offered us; our subjectivity and identities are formed in the definitions of desire held out to us. And our responses to these can be to endorse them, sustain them or reject them. We can never fully escape them.

In short here is the knotty problem of female desire and identity. Women's deepest sense of ourselves is provided by our sense of what we want, what we desire, what we really yearn for. And this, our most crucial sense of ourselves, our desire and our pleasure, has been caught up and mobilised, has been made central in discourses which constantly sustain male power and privileged and female subordination. What my work *Female Desire* attempts to do is move beyond theoretical generalities about the construction of feminity in ideology through to an investigation of what is the lure in the heart of these discourses which causes us to take up and inhabit the feminine position. It is an investigation of how heterosexism and male power gain consent through the workings of desire and pleasure where women perceive their truest sense of themselves. No discussion of ideology or the construction of feminity will be complete without an awareness of the *production* of desire which is so central to the issue of consent to oppressive structures.

Female Desire focusses on dominant representations of desire, mainly because I believe we are all touched by these representations to a greater or smaller degree. Diverse and multiple the workings of desire may be, but the general construction of women ensures that we recognise the call of what is assumed to be female pleasure. It is the focus also because I considered it important to break down the artifical division which has grown up between feminist and non-feminist women. This is a division gleefully inflamed by the media who drive a wedge between feminsts who are said not to understand ordinary women and certainly do not understand pleasure, and ordinary women who know how to follow their truest desires, and correctly treat them as sacrosanct. I wanted to destroy the sacrosanct nature of pleasure, to throw open the contradictions in female desire, to show how we are all, feminists and non-feminists alike, caught in these constructions.

This sort of investigation of female desire is also characteristic of the other, more prevalent treatment of desire within feminism, and it takes me back to my second point. For there is a different, though related way, in which the concept of desire has become a central theoretical focus for some feminists. Parallel to the attempt to analyse the institutions and representations of desire, there has been an attempt to get inside — be more honest and open about — the subjective 'truth' of desire. For while it is important to realise the workings of desire in discourses may be multiple (indeed the 'truth' of desire may be no more than a response to discourse), there remains nevertheless the lived experience that each individual has that there is some subjective truth about our sexual needs and wants, and *that* feeling tends to get covered by the term desire. It is seen as the deep and true expression of our sexual identity. To name our desire might be somehow to name ourselves. And especially with feminists (as with any group which through choice or otherwise, is at a distance from the dominant representations of female desire), there is the pressing question of how far this apparently deep core of ourselves is formed by dominant representations and how far it is 'free' to lead us to real pleasure and satisfaction.

Yet the discussion of this perceived subjective level has proved to be extremely divisive in feminism, almost more divisive than any other issue. Even if the issue has formed the hidden agenda rather than the explicit focus of discussion, fundamentally the divisions have been caused by feminists owning up to our desires, and exploring the questions which desire raises. The first issue which focussed these divisions was, the question heterosexual desire per se, with an initial division between those who discounted the possibility of any "wholesome" heterosexual desire and those who could not. This was followed closely by the issue of pornography and male violence, with an equally explosive division occurring between those who found pornography an unacceptable extension of the violence which women routinely encounter in reality, and those who were more interested in exploring the erotic hold of pornography for women and for men. Close behind came discussions of violence and masochism in sex, those prepared to explore why violence and sex get so closely linked, and those determined to drive a wedge between the mish mash of sex and violence produced by our society.

These issues have proved so explosive that, in England at any rate, feminism is now more frequently experienced in terms of divisions between groups than a sense of shared oppression. In my contention too, some of the subsequent divisions around race and class have built on the divisions and polarties which emerged in the discussions of sexual desire. It is for this reason I make my broader claim that a continued investigation of desire might help shift some of the political impasses and dilemmas which are currently creating such problems for feminism.

In England there have been several publications, some connected with conferences and discussions (some imported from America) which I see as fulfilling at the level of the subjective perception of desire, what I attempt for the general representations of desire, that is, a displacement of the idea of one monolithic female desire, a displacement of the idea that sexual desire can be pinned down to one meaning. Two recently published books give clear expression to these views: they are *Sex and Love*, edited by Sue Cartledge and Joanna Ryan, and *Desire: The Politics of Sexuality* (1982). Here's a typical extract from the collection *Sex and Love*. Responding to a call for a renewed sexual politics where we explore "the experience that lesbians and heterosexuals share and build on this common ground a political understanding of sexuality," Lynn Segal writes,

> "I agree. But what is not indicated here is that what we 'share' is likely to involve all sorts of things we would rather avoid: masochism, self-objectification, domination, guilt, hostility and envy. We must accept and explore these censored emotions, and see how they might conflict with a now fashionably radical but somehow tritely optimistic vision of female eroticism as something powerful and autonomous." (Cartledge & Ryan 1982)

The quote typifies recurrent themes in these writings on desire. They are rarely statements of politically correct desire (whatever that might be!) but instead express a willingness to confess to desire which is erratic, pre-feminist, in particular a call for honesty around the issue of pain, violence and humiliation in sex and a call to talk about this in heterosexual as well as lesbian desire.

Perhaps it seems ironic that I'm claiming this approach is destructive to monolithic conception of desire, when such writing might appear to reinforce the idea of a true desire, fundamental to our sense of selves, merely awaiting confession. But actually the approach to desire is more disruptive than that.

For a start these publications share certain theoretical and political aspirations namely the use of both historical and psychoanalytical theory to dispel the idea of a single meaning which could attach to the sex act. History for example has been used to dispel the idea that "heterosexuality" has one meaning for all time. The act of a woman having sex with a man changes its meanings and implications over history. If the Victorian woman endured heterosexuality as something deriving from men's baser needs, it took the massive work of twentieth century sexologists to introduce the notion of women's *pleasure* into heterosexuality. Which is not to say that women did not enjoy sex — who knows? But rather that women's *desire* within heterosexuality was predominantly a twentieth century construction with all its attendant problems of the psychological oppression to be conducted on women who failed to enjoy sex with men. The question in this is: is it the same act or do you have to look at how it gets its meanings from other acts surrounding it?

It is clear too, that heterosexuality can have different meanings for different class and racial groupings at different historical moments. Equally the appeal to psychoanalytic theory demonstrates also the need to pay attention to the *meanings* surrounding the sexual act, the fact that individual desire is constructed and there can be quite different implications for different individuals within the same sex act. Many of the more personal pieces about individual desire are used precisely in this context to stress the waywardness and often the 'individuality' of desire, without abandoning a sense of the generalities to which female desire is constantly subjected.

These kinds of writings though have opened a real can of worms as far as feminism is concerned. Many women see it as a kind of betrayal, a horrifying confession to all sorts of desires (enjoyment of pornography, enjoyment of masochistic fantasies, pleasure in violent sex) which is seen as a humiliating exposure of a weakness in feminism. It is seen as a sort of failure of feminists to sort out their own lives, and as giving credence to reactionary views that women actually desire and seek out the cruel treatment which men inflict on them. More recently, there has been another question: why not get on with the really important world questions?

So why should I lay grandiose claims for such writing, why should I feel that in such exposures lie the seed for breaking wider political impasses?

I, like many other feminists, feel that these public explorations of the private experiences of desire have a very specific aim. That aim is to counter what I call the 'sexual reductionism' which has settled over feminist discussions of sexuality and has produced such a damaging tone of moralism- with which feminism has now become linked in the public mind. This tone seems to have grown out of a particular interpretation of the feminist tenet, 'the personal is political' which was at one point taken to imply that we can create in our personal (sexual) behaviour a prefigurative way of life, a feminist sexual behaviour. Here is where desire enters; there has been a rampant belief that we could find a feminist desire, that with feminist politics would come a feminist desire, a wholesome desire.

This prescriptive approach is based on an interpretation of the tenet which, put crudely, runs thus: the relations between men and women are determined by the fact that men have social, and economic power over women. This power is reflected in sexual relations themselves and is responsible for the fact that many people do experience *desire* in terms of dominance or submission. Thus when such sadistic or masochistic desires are found (be they in heterosexual or homosexual relations, images or real life, in fantasy or reality) they must be ruthlessly opposed because they help maintain the institution of male dominance. This analysis calls for remedies of personal salvation. Patterns of domination and submission can be broken by giving up relations with men. And if these patterns of desire regrettably crop up in your relations with women, it would be better either to give up sex altogether or struggle on with women but committed to rooting out or repressing any trace of these heterosexist assumptions.

Many women, in response, have taken issue with just how easy and how desirable it would be to prescribe a new form of sexual practice, purged of all the patterns of desire characteristic of oppressive *heterosexual* relations. After all, some women have begun to ask, is sexual *desire* exactly the same as sexual *relations* and if it is not, aren't there ways of changing sexual *relations* without getting onto the quicksand of telling other women what they should or should not be feeling and desiring.

So, against the prescriptive strand there is another- the tendency I am discussing - which returns to an earlier interpretation of the personal is political, that is, as a call to understand how our behaviour is related to external social circumstances, rather than as a prescription for sexual conversion. This approach suggests that if domination and submission appear in relationships — whether in fantasy or the real thing — our first duty is not to stamp it out but to understand what is at stake in such a dynamic, what pleasure it might be bringing and whether this emotional dynamic will inevitably be reflected in our social relations as women. After all unless we understand such structures, how on earth can we understand why they receive such widespread consent.

These issues of course are a lot more raw and controversial than this apparently reasonable exploration of desire. For underneath there lurks a question which may well be heretical to feminism. That question is whether, after all, sexual emotions and sexual fantasy are actually so fatal for our position as women in this society. Is it really the case that if we submit in bed, or in fantasy, to desires of domination and submission desires that are not about sharing, caring, nurturing and equality, will that really invalidate our feminist commitment to end male domination?

This sort of questioning is fraught with dangers. It smacks of a sort of sexual laissez-faire, a tolerance to anything and everything which appears to invalidate feminism's claim that images, attitudes and fantasies (proclaimed by liberalism to be the spontaneous product of the free individual) in fact spring from society's deeply held ideologies about women's inferiority.

This is indeed dangerous ground, but I see no reason to believe that in pursuing this route, British and American feminists are thoughtlessly giving credence to the dominant libertarian view that sex is the private affair of an individual. But dangerous though these ideas might seem we surely stand to gain from them politically. Because beyond what might appear to be a public baring of breasts, and a public tearing of hair for culpable desires, are much more interesting political issues. Firstly there is the fact that in openly exploring desire, desire as contradictory, difficult, formed and contained but important and vital, feminists are turning back towards non-feminist women. In showing this confused and contradictory face, to explore the individual difference in desire, the historical and personal constructions, we are paradoxically in a better position to articulate the problems of all women.

Secondly feminism with its strong clear controversial and often moralistic views of sex is throwing up into the air the issue of desire, and is re-asking the extremely important and pressing question of what exactly is the relationship between personal behaviour, and political movements. And it is my contention that these issues in having previously been taken for granted, have quite regularly caused internal crises within these movements.

One of the great strengths of the initial moments of modern feminism was the revitalising of issues of personal behaviour. Feminism at that period, represented to some extent a stance against the usual left wing morality. On the one hand, feminism took a position against the idea that personal morality was irrelevant, against, e.g. the idea that a man could claim to be sympathetic to feminism yet beat his wife. On the other hand feminists also represented a radical break with the morality of abstinence, the morality which abstained from capitalist pleasures and saw political commitment as one grisly meeting after another. In the place of cynicism or hypocrisy, feminism appeared to offer a politics of political and personal integrity, together with an attention to pleasure and support so blatantly neglected by other movements. In these respects, feminism appeared to be a very different kind of politics already attentive to some of those areas whose neglect has been so crucial in the failure of certain socialist regimes.

But as things have gone on, feminism has almost been hoist with its own petard. When personal morality becomes an element in political discussion, there's room for abuse. Personal 'morality' can very quickly become a metaphor for something else — personal vendettas, political lines, ambitions,

The British feminist movement has recently been rocked by arguments about the correct feminist sexual morality and some women have staked their whole involvement with feminism on the question of sexual practice. It is hard to believe that such divisions have been for the good of all women, or even for the good of feminism. What is more, moralism generates guilt, and we as women are frighteningly susceptible to guilt. An atmosphere of guilt, quite crippling guilt, has been set by some of these discussions.

The discussion of desire is not the indulgence it might appear, it isn't a retreat from thinking about the relation between personal behaviour and social or political forces. It represents an attempt to unpick the tangle of certainties which almost brought feminism to its knees. In the place of a drive for a feminist personal morality, a new question is asked: is personal morality *only* sexual morality? And in the place of prescriptions for a true feminist morality there's a push to debunk sex, to stress the waywardness of sexual desire, to investigate resistances to change rather than offer easy agendas; in short, there's an atmosphere destructive to moralism.

This knocking a simple link between political objectives and personal morality has other implications, a sort of political flip side. Another political scripture might take a knock if these kind of ideas are seen through, there's an implicit challenge to the idea that political authenticity, political progressiveness derives directly from a direct personal experience of oppression. There's an implicit 'deconstruction' of the idea of a direct line of oppression which runs from the economy to the state and ends up in the bedroom with the personal experience of sexual oppression, and then finding its way back as progressive politics. Feminist and socialist politics alike are pretty well synonymous with a struggle against oppression but the proposal of a direct link between personal, experiences of oppression and progressive politics has often been very damaging, it has meant that discussions of politics often end up with attempts to win political arguments by simply proving you are more oppressed than anyone else. Thus within feminism, for example, an experience of being raped or battered within heterosexuality would give a truer political perspective than that generated by an average marriage. Equally, it would leave those whose experience is just ordinary as feeling guilty towards those who had suffered more obviously. A politics based *exclusively* on oppression has got a whole lot of trouble coming to it. At one moment all we can do is be guilty towards those who are more oppressed (politics of solidarity); at the next moment, it has to try to keep people together by pursuading them that there is an alliance between the various oppressions (a problem because the various oppressed groups don't necessarily recognise each other as having similar interests, and a problem because people who see themselves as just 'ordinary' don't recognise themselves in the membership anymore).

It may seem far fetched to suggest a discussion of sexual pleasure contains these implications but it is clear that, certainly around the subject of sexual oppression, some revelations are posing a large question mark. In asserting the pleasure of masochistic submission in, for example, lesbian relations, there is no denial of lesbian oppression or women's subordination to men. However, there is a challenge to the idea that it is the *experience* of oppression through sexual practice which underpins political involvement.

All this could then be pretty heretical to existing political faiths, and while the loss of belief can feel very unsettling the outcome could be a thoroughly good thing. It may become possible to talk about feminism again in terms of attitudes towards friends and work *as well* as sex, and to be able to evolve politics towards women and the family, *and* respond to the pressing issues such as racism — all the issues swamped in the quest for purity of sexual position. It would be pleasingly ironic if, in pursuing an understanding of sex, it should free us from the tyranny of sex.

REFERENCES

Cartledge, Sue and Joanna Ryan (eds.) 1983. *Sex and Love. New Thoughts on Old Contradictions*. London: The Woman's Press.

Coward, Rosalind. 1984. *Female Desire. Women's Sexuality Today*. London: Granada Publishing.

Snitow, Anne., Christine Stangell, Sharon Thompson (eds.) 1982. *Powers of Desire. The Politics of Sexuality*. London: Virago.

BLACK NORTH-AMERICAN WOMEN POETS IN THE SEMIOTICS OF CULTURE

Myriam Díaz-Diocaretz

Introduction

This article is intended as a contribution to reformulate the question of Black North-American poetry and to propose some distinctive features of an area of poetic discourse by women. I will not comment on thematic levels reflecting a woman's perspective nor on aspects of female imagery, for these introduce theoretical complexities outside the domain of this article.

I shall propose a model of analysis which will consider the artistic texts created by Black women poets as part of the socially communicable discourse produced within the mechanisms of North-American culture. Since this project has several dimensions, and may be viewed from more than one perspective, the five aspects I shall refer to are: I. The context of culture and extracultural space in relation to Black North-American poetry. II. The memorizing mechanisms of Black culture. III. Its congenial dialogue with cultural components. IV. The intertextual polemic factor (parody and laughter). Finally, V. Sign provider/sign perceiver interaction in Black poetry.

I shall therefore argue in favour of a critical model that would search first within Black culture itself for the specific aesthetic norms being practised or ignored, rather than for the comparison/contrast method *vis à vis* the norms of the dominant cultural space. This implies that the key elements proposed here could be integrated to the problem of interpretation and verification in Black North-American poetry as a whole.

CULTURE-EXTRACULTURAL SPACE
Some Mechanisms of Exclusion at Work

A study of Black North-American poetry by women (1968 to the present) in the context of the semiotics of culture requires two main preliminary statements. First, as it has been clearly demonstrated in studies of sociolinguistics, Black English, regarded historically, "is different in grammar (in syntax) from the standard American English of the mainstream white culture" (Dillard 1972: 6; see also Himes 1971) therefore it has its own inherent cultural value. Distinctions between both languages frequently coincide with ideological misconceptions from the side of dialectologists and linguists who have aimed at demonstrating a hierarchical linguistic pyramid in which the upper end is British English. This means that the individuality of structure of Black English should not be taken as inferiority as it has normally been considered (Dillard 1972: 5). I believe it unnecessary to insist on redundant justifications on this point, except insofar as it is often considered that the users of Black English speak "incorrectly". While nearly all the women poets write in Black English, none of them does so in an exclusive way. Given the framework of my study I will not establish separations in this sense.

Second, my argument is based not on singular or isolated examples, but on a series of about forty books and chapbooks published in the past decade from around 1968 to the present, by the poets and writers Gwendolyn Brooks, Mari Evans, Nikki Giovanni, Audre Lorde, Alice Walker, June Jordan, and Lucille Clifton (see bibliographical references). It is understood that this synchronic view makes it necessary to touch on some diachronic levels, as the subject for study represents a subgroup in the larger category of Black North-American literature; I will consider the latter not as a literature produced in a minor language, but as a literature created by a so-called minority within a dominant culture.

Poems, as artistic texts, are specific integral verbal signs (Lotman 1975: 62). Artistic texts by Black North-American women contain aesthetic messages with which their creators expand their culture as individuals; from this follows that, by existing textually, they are also part of the Global Sphere of all cultures. In the complex of paradigms of what is roughly known as North-American culture, Black women's poetry has found itself situated in one of the inner spheres, as a silenced, ignored, misinterpreted corpus of texts.

In the exchange of aesthetic messages which is supposed to exist between those who produce signs and those who receive them, we may encounter problems that are significant for the understanding of social semiosis. Between sender and receiver, in Black literature, there has been for a long time a code that is not common to both. Roman Jakobson's proposition is useful. For him, the main problem for discourse analysis is that of the existence of a common code underlying the exchange of messages between sender and receiver (Jakobson 1963). Very often the receiver changes those codes, or does not accept them. In order to understand why a text by a Black poet has many times suffered transference into the category of non-artistic text in mainstream culture because it does not satisfy specific aesthetic requirements, I find it necessary first to realize we have at work here the mechanisms of culture out of which "the minimal unit on any given level" is the opposition "culture-extracultural space" (Lotman 1975: 59-60). Equally important, this phenomenon requires our re-thinking of *who* defines culture and from *which locus*; it demands our re-examination of how this cultural "we" (an individual, a community) as subject of a given delimited sphere, re-defines itself and thereby determines what *is* to be *included* and *excluded* within or without its boundaries.

Culture is a social phenomenon with three major axes facilitating the development of human societies: information, communication, memory. It is a system of signs gathered, ordered, preserved, handed down by a collectivity. Memory, that is, the non-inherited memory of shared experience by a community is manifested by networks of expectations, rules, prescriptions, obligations (Lotman 1975: 66-67; 1979: 71-72). There are many ways in which a collectivity exchanges aesthetic information; one of them is literature.

Some cultures base their existence on the sum of existing texts, and on the different modes in which these are employed: a "textualized culture" considers the text as the model to be imitated. Therefore, what is *not* desirable for imitation is left outside this space. Every culture and its corresponding mechanisms tend towards expansion and extension of its limits. Implicit in the statement of what belongs to culture and what belongs to the extracultural sphere is the antinomy of chaos and order, or organization and non-organization (Lotman 1975). From this general paradigm, a whole series of oppositions are established in this interplay of culture and extracultural space. The culture that speaks to itself and names itself, proclaims itself as such because it places itself as the *positive* member of the oppositions; that is, contemplates itself from the inner point of view. When the "we" of culture speaks and refers to those who do not belong to its sphere, *a paradigmatic set of anomalies* is implied as well (Lotman 1975: 59-60). The extracultural object is then labeled as erroneous, incorrect, insufficient, deviant (in the negative sense). Thus in a standard encyclopaedia of poetry and poetics the realm of anomalies is applied to African literature said to be written in languages of "intuitive syntax", when compared to the literature in Indo-European languages said to be written in "logical syntax" (Preminger 1974: 556). Another case of attributed anomaly is the assumption I pointed out at the beginning of this paper, that Black English is "incorrect".

An even more important example is the contention that Black poetry or a poetry that expresses Blackness (that is, an acknowledged African ancestry, and a perspective from outside the "white" culture) is "not poetry" because it does not follow the culturally accepted normative models established without the participation of, even less the consideration that there might exist, Black aesthetic standards (on denial, rejection, disassociation from culture, see W.E.B. DuBois 1903; Chapman 1968; Henderson 1973; Gayle Jr. 1975; Smith 1980). Or else, that a poetry defining itself as Black or of African heritage is not "universal" (Henderson 1973). This leads to an understanding of the Black writers' insistence that the aesthetics of poetry in the United States is white aesthetics. Further difficulties arise when a Black aesthetics is proposed — and it has happened especially since the 1960's — the theories and propositions continue being integrated into the extracultural space by mainstream criticism. This adds the antinomy of aesthetic/non-aesthetic to be considered critically.

A major opposition we can draw from these and numerous other examples is the hegemony of white as opposed to the more subordinated position of Black literature. Historically speaking, the ancestors of Afro-Northamericans were deprived of their culture of origin and were inserted into a network of mechanisms which has determined for centuries numberless prohibitions, suppressions. Every culture carries out its mechanisms of inclusion and exclusion. We will focus for a moment on some of the important ways in which white culture in the United States has performed exclusion, because it explains, partly, the marginalization — de-territorialization — of the Black woman poet. I refer briefly only to those relevant in this context.

The enforced journey from Africa to the alien shores of North-America — at that time the British Colonies — in the seventeenth century necessarily marks in the history of Black women in a continuum of struggle and in a context of multiple forms of resistance on all levels in a distinctive way (Beal 1975; Davis 1981). Immersed in a social context that cannot be ignored, Black literature emerges from an individual reality which, seen diachronically, consists of at least four modes of existence, or of conditions of life, each one determining corresponding responses for survival.

Many were first uprooted from their African environment and culture, and were sent to places unknown to them from the slave trade market and from there to spend the rest of their lives in bondage; others who were born on slave ships had the same fate (Davis 1971,1981). In this first group we find the author of the first poem by a Black woman slave, Lucy Terry (1730-1821) of Massachusetts, New England, known for her poem "Bars Fight, August 28, 1746," a verse narrative of an Indian raid in Deerfield. Terry celebrates the brave deeds of Samuel Allen and other "valient men" who fought the Indians, called by her "awful creatures".

Phyllis Wheatley, born in Senegal, and sold to a Boston family in 1761, is the second "negro servant" whose poems have been recorded in the history of literature (See J.W. Johnson 1922; Bernikow 1974; E.S. Watts 1977; Hull 1979). Hers was a relatively privileged circumstance because she was brought up in a milieu that encouraged her literacy. In England, where she was sent by her master because of ill-health, she published her only book, *Poems on Various Subjects, Religious and Moral*, received quite positively. Most of those poems were dedicated either to noble people or to prominent bourgeois citizens, and were composed in the Neo-Classical style of Alexander Pope, that is, in the standard accepted literary values of her times. The diction, prosodic and lexical choices in Wheatley's book show a contrast with the covertly encoded subject of being African in a white world. Even though her education induced her to follow the norms of the period — dominated by England — her poems reveal an incipient criticism. She wrote with servitude by providing a code that was common between her and her readers, yet her own sense of de-territorialization did not remain hidden.

It is no historical secret nowadays that the prohibition in every slave-holding state to teach reading and writing to the Africans and their descendants caused a silence of more than a century. This affected not only numberless slaves, but also those who were able to reach freedom by becoming runaways and therefore risking re-capture and most often death. It is only in the late nineteenth century that we can discover traces of poetry by a Black woman.

Among those people born of freed Negro parents who went through different kinds of discrimination is Frances E.W. Harper (1825-1911), a poet who was strongly committed to the antislavery movement, and for whom race was a priority issue. Her book *Poems on Miscellaneous Subjects* (1854), reprinted twenty times, powerfully reflects this (see in particular her texts "A Double Standard", "The Slave Mother", "The Slave Auction", and "Bury Me in a Free Land"). At the beginning of the twentieth century, born of a white father and a black slave mother, Angelina Weld Grimké (1880-1958) has remained almost unknown because her poems have never been collected. Anne Spencer, from Virginia, born in 1882, is another poet still to be discovered. Her poems have never, to my knowledge, been printed in book form (J.W. Johnson 1922). Georgia Douglas Johnson (1886-1966) contributed to the literary production by Black women with two books of poems, *The Heart of a Woman* (1918) and *Bronze* (1922).

Margaret Walker, born in 1915, initiates a period of more visibility for the Black woman poet. With her book *For My People* she won the Yale Younger Poets Award in 1942, the first recognition to be given to a Black woman. Gwendolyn Brooks, (1917) reared in Chicago, marks the beginning of an uninterrupted continuity of Black North-American women's poetic discourse. This history of de-territorialization I have briefly summarized exceeds the bounds of the present survey. However, a context was necessary to explore and to understand how Black women poets enter literature, and how they preserve their own elasticity, their other-languagedness (on this concept see Bakhtin 1978: 294), their distinctness.

To what I have previously described we must add another dimension, valid especially for the synchronic spectrum of poetry written and published since 1968. First, the exclusion of Black poetry until very recently and with very few exceptions in mainstream criticism and related works (biographies, bibliographies, collections of critical essays). Second, the absence of Black women poets in most critical studies from the established criticism, and even from feminist criticism by white women. Third, the limited number of entries on women poets in anthologies including those by Black male editors. Fourth, it is only around 1968 that women poets begin to be published, and in the 1980's that the United States "Third World" presses and publications of women of colour are beginning to make more material available. This is better understood if we remember that only in the late 1960's Black presses and an important number of Black journals were started, among them, the presses Jihad Productions (Newark), Free Black Press (Chicago), Black Dialogue Press (New York), the Journal of Black Poetry Press (California), the magazines *Negro Digest* (later called *Black World*), the *Journal of Black Poetry*, *Soulbook*, *Black Dialogue*, *Liberator*, and *Black Expression*. The establishment of two major Black publishing houses for poetry, Broadside Press of Detroit and Third World Press of Chicago, is significant.

Aware of the North-American's dominant notion of them as a 'mere' minority of African descent not worthy of attention, Black writers and intellectuals become conscious of their need to create their own means of literary production in order to express their views, and to develop their art freely.

After the first presses and journals founded in that decade, some important anthologies were produced by publishing houses from the mainstream of culture. *Black Fire: An Anthology of Afro-American Writings* (1968) edited by LeRoi Jones and Larry Neal, included the work of fifty-seven poets, as well as essays on revolutionary art and literature, "militant" plays, and short stories; all material which makes this book an important document of the decade. Then followed *We Speak as Liberators* (1970), edited by Orde Coombs, conceived to present poetry and art as media for a didactic purpose, and to awaken people and widen perspectives for Afro-American literature; Don Lee's edition of *Dynamite Voices: Black Poets of the 60's* (1971) includes the most representative male poets of that time. All in all, women were still absent in the list of Black revolutionary poets, with the exceptions of Gwendolyn Brooks, Nikki Giovanni, and Sonia Sanchez who begin to have a prominent political or militant voice. Still, it would take a decade for the Black woman poet to be present in a more active manner in the social production of meaning.

White Women's Movement vs. the Black Poet

The relationship between white women and Black women can also be interpreted from the viewpoint of the hierarchical oppositions of culture-extracultural space. In 1970, the collection *The Black Woman: An Anthology* was published, one of the first to include only women, many of whom had never been anthologized before. Toni Cade, its editor, provided in her "Preface" a statement that is quite illustrative of the concerns within the women's movement arising in those years (Cade 1970: 7-12). Speaking of "feminist literature" the writer asks:

> how relevant are the truths, the experiences, the findings of white women to Black women? Are women after all simply women? I don't know that our priorities are the same, that our concerns and methods are the same, or even similar enough so that we can afford to depend on this new field of experts (white, female).
> It is rather obvious that we do not. It is obvious that we are turning to each other (Cade 1970: 9).

Some, Cade concludes, are more concerned with clarifying issues rather than demanding rights; "some demand rights as *Blacks* first, *women* second". The emphasis of turning to each other changed the direction of their writing since that period, and consequently, several poets began to create texts by having an all Black audience or readership in mind. Their art and motivations brought a schism that reinforced the Black women writers' concerns, and it has largely contributed to a more diversified literary productivity in support of a deeper and better understanding of the relationship between poet and society, of what it means to be a Black woman and a poet in the United States (on women's liberation movement and Black women see Beal 1975, and especially Hooks 1981).

In 1979, in "An Open Letter to Mary Daly", Audre Lorde (1979: 94-97) forcefully called attention on an important point of exclusion better understood within the context of the hierarchies of culture. The dismissal of Black women's writings and of their mythology by Mary Daly in her book *Gyn/Ecology* gives ample proof, and Audre Lorde demonstrates it, that the forces of exclusion are still constantly practised among women as well. Lorde's letter states:

> To dismiss our black foremothers may well be to dismiss where european women learned to love. As an african-american woman in white patriarchy, I am used to having my archetypal experience distorted and trivialized but it is terribly painful to feel it being done by a woman whose knowledge so much matches my own. As women-identified women, we cannot afford to repeat these same old destructive, wasteful errors of recognition (Lorde 1979: 95).

Mary Daly's error of recognition represents the particular feminist perspective that confines Black women poets within an additional marginality. New ways of valorization are just in the making in the 1980's. Most recently, in October 1983, Adrienne Rich, speaking about the women's movement in the United States, explains how this movement

> is increasingly being shaped by women of color. The concepts of identity politics, of simultaneity of oppressions, of concrete experience as a touchstone for ideology, the refusal to accept a "room of one's own" in exchange for not threatening the system — these have been explored, expanded on, given voice, most articulately, by women of color, and to say this is not to set up competitions or divisions, but to acknowledge a precious resource, along with an indebtedness, that we can all share (Rich 1983).

In the spheres of what is to be appreciated and what is not appreciated, of what exists and what seems not to exist, of what can be described and what seemingly does not lend itself to description (Lotman 1975: 93-110), Black women poets have constantly been assigned the non-positive side of these antinomies by the dominant sphere of culture. I would like to emphasize that in these antinomies we are not to accept either the positivity or the negativity, but we should be led to consider Black aesthetics and Black literature — I am here expanding Adrienne Rich's words as shown in this context — as part of the sphere of Black culture which is co-existent with other spheres; among them the dominant one is, for political and socioeconomic reasons, the white culture. Both comprise a cultural phenomenon of a wider scope. The hierarchy exists only when seen from within. This is not to deny the issues of oppression determined by the factors of gender, class, race having a strong bearing on identity.

MEMORIZING MECHANISMS:
THE BLACK POET AND THE ALIEN TEXT

While the history of Black North-American literature is relatively short as a culturally existing written discourse, the history of oppression begins, as it is known, three centuries ago. Black poetry has been, as sign, the material with which to re-create, to re-imagine that reality. Afro-Northamerican culture has its own *memorizing mechanisms*, in spite of all the forbidden spheres of human life, in particular the sphere of African songs and rituals, as well as of vital ritual functions such as the prohibitions of dancing, and of the use of drums, which forbade all living corporeality attached to religion (Jahn 1968). These denials were reinforced later by the prohibition of literacy. False or alien theological and legalistic casuistry ultimately forbade language itself (in this case, the African languages of origin). Culture implies memory, not simple remembrance, but the serious goal to relate the individual with each and every experience in the past that it is possible to share with a given community. The functioning modes of the discourse of Black culture have had to advance between the lines and clearly against at least the three principal ways a given culture gives content to its sphere. While the dominant sphere has increased quantitatively its volume of knowledge through publications, it has suppressed that of the Black culture; while it has redistributed its artistic codes by allowing new poetic forms to change the norms and values, it has denied and rejected those from Black texts; and the dominant culture has exerted on Black literature its desire to *forget*, by imposing a deliberate forgetfullness of those declared as non-existent (on the ways a dominant culture functions to extend itself, in order to secure its own continuity, Lotman 1979: 67-135).

The texts by Black North-American poets denounce poetically the multiple cultural confrontations. In the struggle for identity, this kind of literature has managed to preserve, within its own heterogeneity, an internal order. I would like to insist that it is literature which contains their cultural heritage, because "not only do the participants in communication create texts, but the texts also contain the memory of the participants in communication" (Lotman 1975: 74). Let us therefore return to the question of their reworking of their past, as well as to the question of the deep oral tradition shaping the basis for their artistic world.

The poet's attitude with respect to the semiotic context of a culture is perceptible in the modes of integrating other texts (alien texts) into her own writings. Here a distinctive component appears in Black poetry which has not been developed by critics of North-American women's writing. It consists of studying the presence of oral tradition on the one hand, and of the polemic factor on the other, both as part of *intertextual crossings*.

Oral Tradition as Pre-existent Literary Text

Jury Tynianov's (1965) hypothesis that every literary work is built as a double layer of differential rapports, in the first place with the pre-existent literary texts, in the second, with non-literary systems of signification such as the oral languages, is of particular interest for our discussion. Considering the few known exceptions, the pre-existent literary texts of Afro-Northamericans were signs reduced and suppressed; the writing subject was not allowed to make history. The dominant culture muffled the signifying disposition of poetic language, therefore, no socially communicable discourse existed. There are very few texts written and preserved from before the late nineteenth century which could serve to identify the culture; therefore the first rapport mentioned above is scarce in reference to the existing literary texts from the dominant culture. From this follows that, within its own sphere, the *components of oral tradition* fulfill the function of pre-existent texts, of what was preserved, of what continued to circulate orally and which only in the early twentieth century becomes *graphia*.

The Bible Transposed

It is not an unknown fact that the Bible was the major instrument not only to facilitate the literacy of slaves but also to occupy, as a text, all possible areas of knowledge in the consciousness being instructed. Hence the Bible played an enormous role for cultural imposition in Afro-Northamerican culture. This text, however, did not pass freely or untouched from one sphere to the other, because it underwent more than one semiotic transposition. Within the oral tradition, the Bible is the alien text that underlies most often the verbal constructs of slave, religious and secular songs where full lines or longer passages can be identified. By way of example, texts from spirituals and Blues have subsequently been incorporated into contemporary poetry. This means that the Bible traverses oral discourse, passes on to become part of the musical tradition, and from there it comes to be incorporated in poetic discourse. Thus a displacement of the Bible has occurred on many levels and dimensions, all of which need further study. I limit myself to two examples.

Nikki Giovanni's last line "Precious Lord — Take Our Hands — Lead/ Us On" from her poem "Reflections on April 4, 1968" is an adaptation from the title of Thomas A. Dorsey's hymn "Precious Lord, Take My Hand" (for the source I am grateful to Henderson 1973). These are important details to which the responsive reader must be attentive.

Lucille Clifton's books *Good News About the Earth* (1972) and *Two-Headed Woman* (1980) present intertextuality with Christian tradition. Her interpretation of Biblical characters from a Black perspective is a medium to speak out her message to her people: Moses is "an old man leaving slavery"; Delilah is the blessed Black woman; Cain becomes the figure of those who do not respond to Black brotherhood; the poet identifies herself with Mary, the Mother Earth, yet within a revolutionary context. Poems such as "Palm Sunday", "Good Friday", and "Easter Sunday" comprise a vision of faith in the possible transformation of Black people into gods, "if they want it". (Clifton 1972). The cultural dichotomy of being a Black woman brought up in a white Christian tradition produces tensions that are hard to solve, as *Two-Headed Woman* demonstrates. With these two examples I merely intend to suggest that a reading of Black poetry following the varying transformations of the Bible in that particular discourse as nucleus of intertextual crossings, may offer useful interpretive levels to complement the question of the oral tradition which grounds their artistic world.

The Social Text

The Black writers's commitment to safeguard their language and their culture has an increasingly important textual function; this results in the preference for the inclusion of what I shall call *the social text* (Díaz-Diocaretz 1983a, 1984b) whose origin is, in the case of Black poetry, the mainstream of oral tradition. Songs, prayers, enchantments, mythology, all converge on aesthetic effects of rhythm, intonational elements, and even polyphony or heteroglossia: an understanding of the dialogue of languages as it exists in a given era (Bakhtin 1970: 32-80; 1981: 417). From this dialogic verbal construct the writer draws her material.

In the organization of all the possibilities to rebuild a culture which has no written history from the Afro-Northamerican perspective, and in view of the constant expansion of the dominant sphere ("white culture"), the poets are sensitive to the flow of every existing or prospective text from the real, quotidian life, or personal and social contemporary reality; characteristic of this is the proximity to popular spoken language, and of the use of given dates. The latter satisfies the desire to record, to write and re-write their history.

The social text is the previously existent text that brings into poetic discourse the language of the city as messages or parts of messages from the social world. Signs from the street, graffiti, fragments from political documents, testimonies, slave narratives, or references to the discourse of history, and many others. These social texts bring the world closer, make it more familiar for a fearless and freer scrutiny. Equally important are the texts incorporated from the communication media: television advertisements, news from the radio, texts from newspapers. All these give shape to the social context that provokes the writing of the poem. Not every text employed is necessarily taken from actual events (empirical reality). However, if based on an 'imagined' fact, the poet will often support the structure of the poem by conceiving a social text *in the manner of* or *as if* it were real. It is undoubtedly since the 1960's that the social text becomes a characteristic of Black poetry. At the time of the political poetry of the Vietnam period, the social text had already become a common practice for the expression of social criticism and of unrest among Black poets. Sonia Sanchez and Nikki Giovanni are leading voices within this poetic practice.

CONGENIAL DIALOGISM

> "Dialogism is the characteristic epistemological mode of a world dominated by heteroglossia. Everything means, is understood, as part of a greater whole — there is a constant interaction between meanings, all of which have the potential of conditioning others. Which will affect the other, how it will do so and in what degree is what is actually settled at the moment of utterance. This dialogic imperative, mandated by the pre-existence of the language world relative to any of its current inhabitants, insures that there can be no actual monologue."
>
> From "Glossary", Michael Holquist, ed. *The Dialogic Imagination: Four Essays* by M.M. Bakhtin (1981: 426)

Black North-American Music

In addition to the social text, music is an important verbal component in Black poetry (J.W. Johnson 1922). Blues and spirituals provide the rhythmic cadences, the beat, off-beat, the tempo for their free verse. Allusions to titles, songs, quotations, adaptations of song-forms direct the metrical and non-metrical lines (for specific examples of Black poetry in general see Henderson 1973). The lives and the songs of popular musical figures recur in women's poetry (Bessie Smith, Ma Rainey, Mamie Smith, Billie Holliday). Historical and literary Black figures also appear as anthroponimic units and motif for metaphors. Biographies of Black leaders, and facts about victims of the Black Revolution are set as intertextual impulses to give examples of courage, resistance, commitment, and struggle. "A Song of Sojourner Truth" by June Jordan (1980: 49-51) exemplifies the use of both the social text and of music in several of their transpositions. First, it retells Sojourner Truth's story of her defying the laws of racial segregation when she insisted on riding on a bus where she was not allowed. Second, it deals with the life of the ex-slave who later became a heroine in Black culture. Third, it is a poem structured, not according to English diction, but according to the descriptive mode in the 3rd person of the work-song, yet with the "blues logic" of statement and response (on the structure of Blues see Jahn 1968: 166-181). Finally, the rhythmical structure lends itself to a transposition into an actual musical form to the extent that later it was recorded as a song without any modifications of the lexical content (see the recording Jordan & Reagon 1980). Thus the text reclaims its roots of oral heritage.

Longing for Africa: The Missing Sign

Another very crucial intertextual crossing is the mythical, historical, toponymical presence of Africa. Here I must emphasize that Africa, in the poets I have previously mentioned in this synchronic view, represents the desire for reconnection not only with their ancestral past but also with their culture in the present. It is embodied as a rhetorical figure, and it depends on the degree to which each poet related to Africa shows an internal differentiation arising from each individual's desire for connection and also from the orientation of their political concerns.

Africa is, as a text, the sign of the missing culture, an image expressing a certain "intuitive knowledge [...] based on chronological and historical distance; it contains an unsolvable dichotomy for some: the rejection or acceptance of the double heritage" (Brathwaite 1974). The poet's longing for Africa, its unfolding in poetic discourse creates a congenial dialogue within their artistic world. It is the semiotic paradox from which the poet's double consciousness generates, and which permeates the speaker's poetic utterances, outlining another dimension of de-territorialization.

African Spectrum: Seven Glances

The presence of Africa in Gwendolyn Brooks implies an ambivalence of *distancing* and *unifying*; it encompasses the link, by the act of naming herself and naming Africa in relation to the individual "('MY NAME IS AFRIKA.'/Well, every fella's a Foreign Country./This Foreign Country speaks to you.)" (Brooks 1970: 15). Africa is a reality of separation and estrangement.

In June Jordan's work we witness the sexual, physical, political, and economic violations as they intersect in the speaker who is simultaneously Africa and the Black woman. The constant referent to the destructive exploitation of human and natural resources for the benefit of a few is extended to serve as metaphor for the oppressed peoples of the world.

Nikki Giovanni explores the differences between Africans and Black North-Americans; two worlds that are "bounded by difference/for nothing is the same except oppression and shame." (Giovanni 1975). Yet both may come together if they accept the possibilities of struggle and of dreaming of freedom together. This was Giovanni's central idea with respect to Africa during the 1960's, and the 1970's.

In Mari Evans, Africa resounds as the dream of Nationhood, as the Oneness of Black people regardless of time and distance. While for Nikki Giovanni shattered pride and domination are the only common experience, for Mari Evans it is a common hatred and the ancient past that serve as motivations to become unified. Evans believes strongly that as a Black woman she must identify the enemy and refuse to be part of destruction. To identify the enemy is also to establish her own boundaries, to choose to stay on the margins and from there to fight.

Alice Walker focuses on the clash of the two cultures that are put face to face in the encounter of the Black North-American woman in Africa. She finds no points of connection between herself and the native Africans. The attempts the speaker makes to be part of the African world fail.

In Lucille Clifton's *Good Times: Poems* (1969) the reader is offered images of Africa that are common in Black poetry in the United States: the sign of the past, in which slave-ships and slaves themselves represent the unconnected, the rootless beings still adrift between Africa and North America (1969: 20). By contrast, the most integrated vision of Africa appears in Audre Lorde's *The Black Unicorn* (1978). Lorde incorporates cultural African elements in the creation of her poetic world, ancient and contemporary. African religion and the rituals of West African women are juxtaposed to her own experience as an Afro-Northamerican lesbian feminist, and work as backbone in her image-making; not in the background but as an organic poetic reality. Facing her present culture, Lorde turns to her own goddesses for energy and embarks in her quest for identity as a fully empowered being.

Therefore, Africa as a *locus* for rediscovery and political reflection is explored in a wide spectrum among these poets. It represents the act of looking back from the margin to another margin that functions historically and culturally as a sign, a mask of double exclusion, and which comprises their dual culture. The poet's marginality is not simply a geographical de-territorialization. It is a political, ethical, and personal territory that they seek to reclaim; simultaneously, they decide to face and confront the marginator. With self-assertion as the main cry for survival since around 1965 (when the main text was the paradigm "Black is beautiful") and with the insistence on self-identity, the poets refuse to become part of what has rejected them and thereby re-territorialize themselves and their culture, now on their own terms (Díaz-Diocaretz 1980, 1982, 1984a).

INTERTEXTUAL POLEMIC FACTOR

The oral tradition, the Bible, the social text, Black music, and Africa are some of the strategies used by the poets to support their verbal message, textual devices incorporated as the memorizing mechanisms of Black culture. If we have to offer a synchronic explanation, it is with the purpose of tracing the tradition in its own sources: oral discourse. We cannot ignore the important relationship of these poets with the United States society, a component leading to another significant differentiative category. We have seen that the poets create arguments for a dialogue with their own culture, by integrating the social texts into their ideological world vision. Yet, a significant part of those social texts are integrated to prepare and to build a network of polemic with the white establishment. The antinomies between the Black speaker and the oppressor or between the Black poet and authoritative social and cultural canons result in an intertextual polemic between the two cultures and each corresponding set of aesthetic norms.

Against the Forces of the Oppressor's Codes

The intertextual nettings in the poetry of Black North-American women are woven by a plurality of polemics. It is important to distinguish the specificity of this polemic factor from the one in non-Black literature. Although there are analogies with, for instance, feminist poetic discourse since the alien text is used in a double sense and can be included to express irony (Díaz-Diocaretz 1983a, 1983b, 1984b), Black women's polemic is translinguistic and transcultural.

The major polemic aims at the standard literary language and its conventions, and at the restriction which those instill on the texts. If poetry *per se* violates the norms of a given literary language (Mukarovsky 1977: 9), then the Black poet in the United States breaks the boundaries twice. The poets have sought their linguistic material in lexical spheres far away from the canonical standards of beauty or else they have been indifferent to them, consequently they have negated them (on negation of standard norms see Mukarovsky 1977). From the colloquial situation in the street, to the directness of bare phrases to produce a personal or collective dialogue, the Black poet has no limits or self-restricted norms.

Humour, Parody, Laughter as Cultural Transgressions

Closely related to the polemic against the forces of the oppressor's codes pointed at the literary language and norms, there is yet another aspect of polemic worthy of closer study, consisting of the frequent juxtaposition of conversational or informal speech with formal written language, a device that might be considered as a type of code-switching, as defined by Labov (1972). The primacy of written over spoken language in relation to prestige varieties of communication is constantly transgressed; more than that, it is a transgression that often gives rise to the parody of dominant standards because it creates a reversal of the ground rules. This peculiarity has several dimensions. If we keep in mind that the texts are brought forth against the forces of the oppressor's codes, we can contextualize irony, sarcasm, and plain humour (also common in Black musical tradition) as part of the polemic with the dominant culture. As a textual strategy, it produces a chain of poetic devices, and presupposes for the speaker and addressee — and, in a larger framework, for the poet and the reader — not only a kind of common referential knowledge, but also a certain familiarity or a collective intimacy among the interlocutors based on a common reservoir of received ideas. Distance disappears. A freer contact between the truth or reality and the object of discourse takes the place of norms (Bakhtin 1970: 181). This type of ironic humour is parallel to *le rire carnavalesque* of oral discourse of folk festivities (Bakhtin 1968:5) consisting of the use of popular idioms, sayings, proverbs, curses, comic verbal compositions, sacred, non-sacred rituals, and also swearwords, all of which help the poet to carry out the 'profanation' and 'desacralization' of the accepted canons. In other instances, it may simply be the reversal of accepted norms, of stereotypes. Let us consider a few examples of this parodic carnival laughter which is, in Black poetry, of ideological motivation.

Cursing and onomatopoeic devices are consciously verbalized social forms of folk humour. In "verse from a fragmentary marriage" by June Jordan (1980: 39):

>   midtown manhattan
>   honk
>   beep
>   piss
>   shit
>   buzzbuzz
>   buzzbuzz
>   you
>   all over my mind and eyes
>
>   lilacs in starlight
>
>   midnight manhattan
>   you
>
>   all over
>   all over
>
>   for a while

By Jordan (1980: 36), another parodic poem, "Sketching in the Transcendental":

>   Through the long night the long trucks running the road
>   The wind in the white pines does not ululate like
>   that

> Nor do the boreal meadowlands the mesopotamia
> of the spirit does not sing
>
> the song of the long trucks
>
> The spirit differs
> from a truck
>
> a helluva lot

or Alice Walker's poem XXIV, from the series of forty-five brief texts called "African Images: Glimpses from a Tiger's Back" (1968: 3-16), in which she reverses a stereotype: an African child becomes scared of the speaker's white friend because she believes that he 'wants her For his dinner'.

SIGN PROVIDER/SIGN PERCEIVER INTERACTION

Let us now touch upon several artistic features related to the above. Complicity in language and other-languagedness acquire a relationship with the ongoing event of current life whereby speaker and addressee are intimately participating. I will concentrate briefly on the speaker/addressee speech act interaction, an aspect which can hardly be overestimated in Black poetry because it creates a radically new zone. I suggest a consideration of this factor not following the rigid notions of a pragmatics using sentences destitute of context, but taking into account each poem as a situational and linguistic verbal complex.

The act of reading is a dialectic phenomenon requiring the interpretive cooperation between author and reader through the text (Eco 1976,1979). A poem, as an artistic text, is a "sign mediating between two individuals, and like every sign it needs two subjects for the fulfillment of its semiotic function: the one who provides the sign and the one who perceives it" (Mukarovsky 1977: 163). From specific textual strategies we can delineate the possible horizon of texts as a whole, and draw the type of perceiver/ receiver the poet envisions. The very choice of writing in Black English is indicative of the intended addressee, and the degrees to which the uses of Black English varies — whether used predominantly or seldom — marks distinctions among poets from the point of view of speaker/addressee interaction, and may also help to detect certain discontinuities in the trajectory of a single poet. It explains, for example, the reception of Gwendolyn Brooks's books before 1968 mainly by a white readership because she did not pretend "to speak for a people" (Kunitz 1950: 52-56). In *Riot* (1969) Brooks shifts her perspective radically from speaking *about* her people to addressing her people directly.

In the 1960's Black North-American writers experienced a changing cohesiveness along with the Neo-African world movement's new consciousness; with this change came the development of what was known as Black Revolutionary poetry. It became a priority to define their identity as a people, and they fully acknowledged the necessity to write guided by a responsibility of the individual towards his/her community. The motto "Black art must expose the enemy, praise the people and support the revolution" (from *New Black Poetry*) was a common attitude in the 60's and 70's. It is in this context that the Black woman poet emerges in contemporary literature.

The poetic persona provides the passage through which the consciousness of the poet is perceived. Black women poets rarely step out of their own cultural history: they identify with and define the female self as speaker to encompass the experience of the Black woman as the axes where the individual and the collective converge. This trait is clearly not a deficiency, but an implicit commitment to their own cultural territory and their struggle. The paradigm "I am a Black woman" is not simply one of individual limits. The poets in their self-assertion, self-determination, and self-affirmation also formulate the attempt to become a collective voice. This explains that a significant number of poems are addressed to a Black readership.

However, the speaker/addressee interaction is not merely related to who speaks and to whom. The reader will recognize images or utterances linked in an oral, discoursive fashion, from which ideological oppositions can be extracted: We/They, Black/White, Black/NonBlack, Master/Slave, Obedience/Rebellion, Freedom/Bondage. Speaker and addressee establish meaningful oppositions and correlations between pairs of opposing terms. One cultural value opposes the other. I provide an example from Nikki Giovanni that synthesizes some of these correlations: "If white defines Black and good defines evil then men/define women or women scientifically speaking describe/men" (1975: n.p.). Speech is directly linked with revolt. The poets' messages are not casual metaphorical formulations. For these poets, to speak is to take responsibilities for the encircled "us", for the clearly defined "my people". If the poem is read according to the codes in which they have been designed, speaker and addressee become equally involved in the practice of social and poetic meaning. Such are the ways to re-territorialize language and the individual.

Black women's poetry can be spoken in a familiar, fearless tone; the poets aim at freeing their speakers and addressees from the pitifully serious tones of supplication, lament, humility, and piousness, as well as from the menacing speech act of intimidation, from the prohibitions instilled by authoritative hierarchic and patriarchal discourse. This is one of the boldest experiments and achievements in North-American literature of the past decades.

REFERENCES

1. Sources

Brooks, Gwendolyn. 1945. *A Street in Bronzeville*. New York: Harper and Row.
-----. 1956. *Bronzeville Boys and Girls*. New York: Harper.
-----. 1960. *The Bean Eaters*. New York: Harper.
-----. 1963. *Selected Poems*. New York: Harper and Row.
-----. 1968. *In the Mecca: Poems*. New York: Harper and Row.
-----. 1969. *Riot*. Detroit: Broadside Press.
-----. 1970. *Family Pictures*. Detroit: Broadside Press.
-----. 1971. *Aloneness*. Detroit: Broadside Press.
-----. 1971. *Annie Allen*. Westport, Conn.: Greenwood Press.
-----. 1975. *Beckonings*. Detroit: Broadside Press.
Clifton, Lucille. 1969. *Good Times: Poems*. New York: Random House.
-----. 1972. *Good News About the Earth: New Poems*. New York: Random House.
-----. 1974. *An Ordinary Woman*. New York: Random House.
-----. 1980. *Two-Headed Woman*. Amherst: University of Massachusetts Press.
Evans, Mari. 1968. *Where Is All the Music?*. London: Paul Breman. Heritage Series, VI.
-----. 1970. *I Am a Black Woman*. New York: Morrow.
-----. 1974. *I Look at Me!*. Chicago: Third World Press.
Giovanni, Nikki. 1968. *Black Judgement*. Detroit: Broadside Press.

-----. 1970. *Black Feeling, Black Talk / Black Judgement*. New York: William Morrow and Co.
-----. 1970. *Poem of Angela Yvonne Davis*. New York: Afro Arts.
-----. 1970. *Re:Creation*. Detroit: Broadside Press.
-----. 1971. *Spin a Soft Black Song: Poems for Children*. New York: Hill and Wang.
-----. 1972. *My House: Poems*. New York: William Morrow and Co.
-----. 1973. *Ego Tripping and Other Poems for Young People*. New York: L. Hill.
-----. 1975. *The Women and the Men*. New York: William Morrow and Co.
-----. 1976. *Gemini: An Extended Autobiographical Statement on My First Twenty-Five Years of Being a Black Poet*. New York: Penguin Books.
-----. 1980. *Cotton Candy on a Rainy Day*. New York: Morrow Quill Paperbacks.
Jordan, June. 1969. *Who Look at Me*. New York: Crowell.
-----. 1971. *Some Changes*. New York: Dutton.
-----. 1977. *Things That I Do in the Dark: Selected Poetry*. New York: Random House.
-----. 1980. *Passion: New Poems, 1977-1980*. Boston: Beacon Press.
----- and Bernice Reagon. "For Somebody To Start Singing". Poems and Lyrics by J. Jordan, music by B. Reagon. Washington D.C.: Watershed Tapes, 1980.
Lorde, Audre. 1968. *The First Cities*. New York: The Poets Press.
-----. 1970. *Cables to Rage*. London: Paul Breman. Heritage Series, IX.
-----. 1973. *From a Land Where Other People Live*. Detroit: Broadside Press.
-----. 1975. *New York Head Shop and Museum*. Detroit: Broadside Press.
-----. 1976. *Coal*. New York: W.W. Norton.
-----. 1978. *The Black Unicorn: Poems*. New York: W.W. Norton.
Walker, Alice. 1968. *Once: Poems*. New York: Harcourt, Brace and World.
-----. 1973. *Revolutionary Petunias and Other Poems*. New York: Harcourt, Brace and Jovanovich.

2. General

Bakhtin, Mikhaïl. 1968. *Rabelais and His World*. Trans. Hélène Iswolsky. Cambridge, Mass.: M.I.T. Press.
-----. 1970. *La poétique de Dostoievsky*. Trans. Isabelle Kolitcheff. Paris: Editions de Seuil.

-----. 1978. *Esthétique et théorie du roman*. Trans. Daria Olivier. Paris: Editions Gallimard.

-----. 1981. *The Dialogic Imagination: Four Essays*. Ed. Michael Holquist, trans. Caryl Emerson and M. Holquist. Austin and London: University of Texas Press.

Beal, Frances M. 1975. "Slave of a Slave No More: Black Women in Struggle." *The Black Scholar* 6/6 (March). Rpt. 12/6 (November/December 1981): 16-24.

Bernikow, Louise, ed. 1974. *The World Split Open: Four Centuries of Women Poets in England and America, 1552-1950*. New York: Random House (Vintage Books).

Brathwaite, Edward Kamau. 1974. "The African Presence in Caribbean Literature." *Daedalus* 2 (Spring): 73-109.

Cade, Toni, ed. 1970. *The Black Woman: An Anthology*. New York: New American Library (Mentor Book).

Chapman, Abraham, ed. 1968. *Black Voices: An Anthology of Afro-American Literature*. New York: New American Library (Mentor Book). "Introduction": 21-49.

Coombs, Orde, ed. 1970. *We Speak as Liberators: Young Black Poets*. New York: Dodd, Mead and Co.

Davis, Angela. 1971. "Reflections on the Black Woman's Role in the Community of Slaves." *The Black Scholar* 3/4 (December). Rpt. 12/6 (November/December 1981): 2-15.

-----. 1981. *Woman, Race & Class*. New York: Random House.

Díaz-Diocaretz, Myriam. 1980. "*Passion* by June Jordan", *Thirteenth Moon* V, 1 & 2: 147-155.

-----. 1982. "*Black Sister: Poetry by Black American Women, 1746-1980*", *Thirteenth Moon* VI, 1 & 2: 137-143.

-----. 1983a. *Reading and Writing in the Act of Translation: The Poetry of Adrienne Rich*. Ph.D. diss. State University of New York at Stony Brook. Ann Arbor: University Microfilms International.

-----. 1983b. "Homosocial Arrangements: From Concept to Discourse", in *Among Men, Among Women: Sociological and Historical Recognition of Homosocial Arrangements*, ed. Mattias Duyves et al. Amsterdam: Sociologisch Instituut, Univ. of Amsterdam: 441-449.

-----. 1983c. "Een brug slaan tussen vertalen en vrouwenstudies". Trans. R. Lemaire, in *Kongresbundel: Winteruniversiteit Vrouwenstudies*. Nijmegen: 52-57.

-----. 1984a. "Black North-American Voices: The Poetry of G. Brooks, L. Clifton, M. Evans, N. Giovanni, A. Walker and J. Jordan" Limited edition. Leeuwarden, The Netherlands: Lesbisch Archief.
-----. 1984b. *The Transforming Power of Language: The Poetry of Adrienne Rich*. Utrecht: HES Uitgevers.
Dillard, J.L. 1972. *Black English: Its History and Usage in the United States*. New York: Random House.
DuBois, W.E.B. 1903. *The Souls of Black Folk: Essays and Sketches*. Chicago: McClurg. Crest paperback, 1961.
Eco, Umberto. 1976. *A Theory of Semiotics*. Bloomington: Indiana University Press.
-----. 1979. *The Role of the Reader: Explorations in the Semiotics of Texts*. Bloomington: Indiana University Press.
Ferris, William. 1979. *Blues from the Delta*. Garden City, New York: Doubleday.
Gayle Jr., Addison. 1975. "Introduction", in *The Forerunners: Black Poets in America*, ed. Woodie King Jr. 1981. Washington, D.C.: Howard University Press.
Henderson, Stephen. 1973. *Understanding the New Black Poetry: Black Speech and Black Music as Poetic References*. New York: William Morrow & Co.
-----. 1975. "Saturation: Progress on a Theory of Black Poetry" *Black World* (June): 4:17.
Himes, E., ed. 1971. *Pidginization and Creolization of Languages*. Cambridge: Cambridge University Press.
Hooks, Bell. 1981. *Ain't I a Woman: Black Women and Feminism*. Boston, MA.: South End Press.
Hull, Gloria T. 1979. "Afro-American Women Poets: A Bio-Critical Survey", in *Shakespeare's Sisters: Feminist Essays on Women Poets*, ed. Sandra M. Gilbert and Susan Gubar. Bloomington: Indiana University Press: 165-182.
Jahn, Janheinz. 1968. *Neo-African Literature: A History of Black Writing*. Trans. Oliver Coburn and Ursula Lehrburger. New York: Grove Press.
Jakobson, Roman. 1963. *Essais de linguistique générale*. Paris: Minuit.
Johnson, James Weldon, ed. 1922. *The Book of American Poetry*. New York: Harcourt Brace Jovanovich.
Kunitz, Stanley. 1950. "Bronze by Gold". *Poetry* 76: 52-56.
Labov, William. 1972. *Sociolinguistic Patterns*. Philadelphia: University of

Pennsylvania Press.

Lorde, Audre. 1979. "An Open Leter to Mary Daly" in *This Bridge Called My Back: Writings by Radical Women of Color.*, ed. Cherríe Moraga & Gloria Anzaldúa. Watertown, MA,: Persephone Press. 1981: 94-97.

Lotman, Jury. et al. 1975. "Theses on the Semiotic Study of Cultures (As Applied to Slavic Texts)" in *The Tell-Tale Sign: A Survey of Semiotics*, ed. Thomas A. Sebeok. Lisse/Netherlands: The Peter de Ridder Press: 57-84.

-----. 1979. *Semiótica de la Cultura*. Madrid: Cátedra.

Mukarovsky, Jan. 1977. *The Word and the Verbal Art: Selected Essays*. Trans. and ed. John Burbank & Peter Steiner. New Haven: Yale University Press.

Preminger, Alex, ed. 1974. *Princeton Encyclopaedia of Poetry and Poetics*. Princeton, New Jersey: Princeton University Press (Enlarged Edition).

Rich, Adrienne. 1983. "Speech delivered at Women in Struggle: Seneca, Medgar Evers, Nicaragua" evening sponsored by IKON magazine, October 28. *Womanews* (December).

Smith, Barbara. 1980. *Toward a Black Feminist Criticism*. New York: Out & Out Books.

Tynianov, Juiry. 1965. "De l'évolution littéraire" (1927). In *Théorie de la littérature*, ed. T. Todorov. Paris: Seuil.

Watts, Emily Stipes. 1977. *The Poetry of American Women from 1632 to 1945*. Austin: University of Texas Press.

PRACTICAL CRITICISM: LAW, RACISM AND ART

WOMEN'S RIGHTS AS HUMAN RIGHTS: LATIN AMERICAN COUNTRIES AND THE ORGANIZATION OF AMERICAN STATES (OAS)

Cecilia Medina

Women and Latin America.

As a starting point it is important to specify that in this work the term Latin America is used for those countries in the American continent whose mother tongue is Spanish, Portuguese or French (Argentina, Bolivia, Brazil, Colombia, Costa Rica, Cuba, Chile, Dominican Republic, Ecuador, El Salvador, Guatemala, Haiti, Honduras, Mexico, Nicaragua, Panama, Paraguay, Peru, Uruguay and Venezuela). The term is not meant to imply that these countries are a unit. The differences among them in social, political and economic status are sometimes considerable. For that matter, it could even be argued that each country could hardly be called a unit, as the social and economic differences of the individuals living in them are also immense. These facts must be taken into account whenever the term is used in this paper.

It is a well-known fact that the feminist movement is one of the movements striving for a fairer and more humane world. The struggle for equal rights for women is a struggle for the recognition of, and respect for, one of the premises upon which human rights are based, namely that all human beings are free and equal before the law, and that nothing justifies discrimination on the basis of any characteristics generally attributed to a group. Such discrimination would contravene the essence of human rights, which may be broadly defined as claims advanced by individuals within the human community "which are possessed by virtue of being human" (Levine, 1980: 137; Universal Declaration of Human Rights, Preamble). As a logical consequence of the fact that women's rights are human rights, feminism, in theory, is a movement to achieve a democratic society, without which human rights may not be fully enjoyed. The aim it pursues is more than the mere formal representative democracy which often enough begins and ends with elections. For historical reasons, women have a first-rate experience to recognize between formal and real equality, and to realize that political power is not only exercised by the state but that it also affects inter-personal relations.

These goals make the struggle of Latin American women a particularly difficult one. A significant number of Latin American countries have seldom experienced even formal democracy, and no one can deny that dictatorships in that continent are not the best of soil for human rights in general, and for equal rights for women in particular. To the fact that they depend for their survival on force and arms, it should be added that their ideologies oppose the equality of the sexes; therefore, the struggle for women's rights is considered by many Latin American dictatorships as a frontal attack to their social organization, and the demands for women's rights are at best ignored and at worst repressed.

In this schematic review of social and political pressures which affect the feminist movement, we must add the fact that Latin American countries have a tendency to political polarization. The role women occupy within the family as mother and housewife is part of the right-wing ideology, whereas the left-wing normally asserts that the main contradiction is between social classes and not between the sexes, and once that is resolved there will be no need to fight for equality of the sexes because it will come as a consequence of the transfer of political power and of social and economic transformations. In respect with this assertion it seems important to stress that to struggle for women's rights does not mean — as some would contend — the weakening of the political and social struggles to change society as a whole. Much to the contrary, historical experience suggests that whenever women from the lower and middle classes abandon their traditional role and become aware of public life, the probabilities that they undergo a positive political transformation, from conservative stands to progressive stands, increase considerably. This is an area which should be studied further in Latin America.

It would give the feminist movement important elements for its struggle if an answer would be provided to questions such as whether women have indeed abandoned their traditional role when confronted with exceptional periods in their countries (wars, revolutions, serious breaks of social order); if so, which roles they have actually played; and whether this change in roles has been temporary and limited to the areas strictly needed to overcome the exceptional situation, or, on the contrary, whether the change has been broader than that and of a more permanent nature.

The role women have played in the Cuban and the Nicaraguan revolutions, and the consequences that it might have had once the military part of the revolution was over, would constitute an important subject for study. I am not aware if, for example, someone has studied the possible relation between the increase in women's vote for the coalition of parties which supported the Allende government in March 1973, and the fact that before the election women had organized the distribution of food and other goods in their neighbourhoods, to counteract part of the effects of the destabilization campaign carried out at the instigation, and with the help of, the US government. Within those organizations (called in Chile *Juntas de Abastecimiento y Control de Precios*) women had a first-hand experience of responsibilities outside their homes and began to realize the effect of politics (a topic that many Latin American women understand as men's concerns) in their daily lives. The study of another experience lived in Chile in the three years of the Allende government would perhaps help prove the point from another angle, that is, that the traditional role of women in society is a negative factor for progressive political, economic and social change. (See Mattelart, 1975) A Chilean upper-class women's movement called *El Poder Femenino* (Feminine Power) orchestrated a campaign to convince women that it was their duty to fight Allende in order to protect their proper role in society, namely that of mothers and housewives. They emphasized the danger of losing their children to the state (or worse, to Russia or Cuba) and underlined the enormous problems to procure food and other basic products, caused to a significant extent by the US government destabilization campaign and carried out among others by these same upper class women of *El Poder Femenino*. The campaign proved fruitful since it was based on two major concerns — motherhood and sustenance. Many women from the middle and lower classes, who would not benefitiate by having Allende's government replaced by a military *coup* were convinced by these arguments and fought Allende and his political coalition. At the same time, *El Poder Femenino* incited women to appeal for male virility and their duty to defend their families (See *Revolución*, 1978: 6-12). These examples suggest that in Latin American countries the achievement of equality that will permit women to be incorporated into public life is, more than merely a step forward towards the objective of a real and substantial change in society so many are fighting for, a necessary step without which that change cannot be achieved.

Latin American legal provisions regarding women.

Aside from this negative social and political framework, in many — if not all — Latin American countries, the legal framework is blatantly discriminatory against women. Since one of the first stages in the struggle for human rights is that of setting forth non-discriminatory, impersonal and thus general, legal norms establishing equality and the corresponding judicial remedies to safeguard it, I will first briefly summarize the domestic legal provisions in various Latin American countries regarding women, in order to illuminate one field of action for Latin American feminist movements. Undoubtedly the struggle does not exhaust itself in this stage. The *recognition* of rights must be followed by their *implementation*. Here the struggle aims at having legal mechanisms devised to ensure the people that the rights granted will be real as well as formal. These mechanisms will vary according to the obstacles encroaching upon human rights, which in their turn will depend on the kind of social and economic structures within which they operate (tax laws, social security system, regulation of property, affirmative action). It is clear that legal provisions will not necessarily lead to changes in conduct, but it is a fact that where the rule of law prevails, even if only partially, legal norms do legitimize claims. It is also evident that not all these legal changes are possible to be achieved now in Latin America, but at least the stage of suppression of specific inequalities should be achievable under the present circumstances.

From the twenty countries constituting Latin America, in the present study Cuba has been left aside for reasons of insufficient information. As to the rest, the data available did not cover all the fields studied. Some of the information was not taken from primary but from secondary sources (CIM, 1982). Consequently this work does not pretend to be exhaustive, and further studies should be carried out to obtain an accurate and complete view of the legal status of women in Latin America.

In the description that follows I have considered as basic elements the way family and marriage are regulated in constitutional and in civil law, the treatment of certain conducts in criminal law (adultery, abortion, rape), and the position of women in labour law (protective legislation). The provisions chosen offer good examples to give a general panorama of the legal discrimination of women.

The constitutions.

An adequate place to begin with is the provisions in the constitutions which regulate family and marriage, constitutions being the supreme laws upon which all other norms rest and to which all other norms must conform. The constitutions of sixteen countries (Bolivia, Brazil, Costa Rica, Chile, Dominican Republic, Ecuador, El Salvador, Guatemala, Haiti, Honduras, Nicaragua, Panama, Paraguay, Peru, Uruguay and Venezuela) (See Peaslee, 1970; Chile, 1981), take provision on the family, matrimony and motherhood stating that the family is an essential element of society and matrimony a basis, sometimes and essential basis, of the family (Costa Rica, art. 52). The Chilean constitution of 1980 goes as far as declaring illegal "all acts by people or groups which propagate doctrines aimed against the family...", convictions on offences of this type resulting in a five-year suspension of the rights to vote and to be elected to public office and a ten-year suspension of several other rights, such as the right to work in certain areas (educational establishments, mass media, the administration) and of the right to participate as leaders in political, community or trade organizations (Art. 8).

Civil law.

Let us briefly summarize what kind of family relations these constitutions proclaim as an essential element of society. The legal provisions speak for themselves.

a) In ten countries a married woman's domicile and residence is that of the husband. Women are often obliged to follow their husbands wherever they go, unless serious injury to the woman might follow. It is a judge who decides what may be a serious injury (Civil Codes (CC) arts.: Argentina: 90 (9), 186; Brazil: 36, 233; Chile: 71, 136; Ecuador: 135; El Salvador: 69, 183; Panama: 83, 112; Peru: 24, 162; Haiti: 195; Honduras: 7; Venezuela: 33, 138).

b) In nine countries the community in property that arises or may arise as a result of marriage is administered by the husband (CC arts.: Argentina: 1276; Brazil: 233; Chile: 1718, 1749, 1752; Ecuador: 139; Guatemala: 131; Haiti: 1206; Panama: 1192; Peru: 188, 170, 161, 169; Venezuela: 148, 168 and 170). In three countries a married woman may not administer her own property or may do it with limitations. It is the husband's right to administer it (CC arts.: Chile: 1749; Haiti: 1206; Ecuador: 157).

c) In eight countries a husband may object to his wife working outside the home and may have her judicially prevented from doing so (CC arts.: Argentina: 190; Brazil: 247; Chile: 150; Guatemala: 113, 114; Mexico: 168, 169, 170; Peru: 173; Venezuela: 140. Bolivia's Family Code: 98, 99). In five countries it is an explicit legal obligation of the marriage contract that the woman shall care for her children and shall "supervise" domestic work (CC arts.: Brazil: 240; Mexico: 168; Guatemala: 110; Peru: 161. Bolivia's Family Code: 98).

d) In four countries, one of the woman's legal obligations set forth in the contract of marriage is to obey the husband (CC arts.: Chile: 131; Ecuador: 134; El Salvador: 182; Haiti: 197, 198).

e) Marriage alters the legal capacity of women in four countries. One important consequence thereof is that she may not enter into any contract by herself but has to be represented by her husband. To avoid practical problems that would certainly arise from this situation, the law "presumes" the husband's consent in certain contracts such as that of buying groceries (CC arts.: Argentina: 188, 189; Brazil: 233, 242 II, 247, 247 III; Chile: 132, 136, 137, 147, 159; Venezuela: 140). In two countries this legal capacity is so curtailed that husbands have a marital *potestas*, that is to say, a right over the *person* and *property* of the wife (CC arts.: Chile: 132; Paraguay, art. 1 of Law 236 of 6 September 1954).

f) Nine countries confer the *patria potestas*, that is, the right a parent has over the person and property of a son or daughter, to the father, or give the father's opinion priority when the *patria potestas* is granted to both parents[1] (CC arts.: Argentina: 264; Brazil: 233, 384, 385; Chile: 240, 247; El Salvador: 230, 252; Mexico: 426, 427; Panama: 192; Peru: 391, 392, 421; Venezuela: 261 (2), 272, 59. Costa Rica's Family Code: 138).

g) Among those countries accepting divorce, with or whithout dissolution of the legal bond of marriage, six consider adultery of the wife as a cause thereof. A husband may give cause for divorce only when he keeps a woman other than his wife and when this is done with public scandal, or in the marital residence, or abandoning the wife (CC arts.: Chile: 171; Haiti: 268; Honduras: 143; Panama: 114; Venezuela: 184, 185; El Salvador: Chapter V). Sometimes, once divorce proceedings are started, the judge may order that the wife be placed in an "honest" house (CC arts.: Argentina: 205; El Salvador: 150; Honduras: 196).

Criminal law.

However, it is in criminal law where the true image of the Latin American "social woman" emerges. The fact that woman's sexuality can only be exercised within the legal bond of marriage, and her submission in this respect to husband, father or brother appear crystal-clear. In order to understand fully the discrimination present in the provisions, it is relevant to point out that in criminal law the degree of punishment for an offence depends upon the *value being protected* (life, physical integrity, privacy, property) and upon the *circumstances* in which the offence is perpetrated; the degree of moral evil involved in the offence is relevant to the gradation of punishment. The following examples are almost self-explanatory.

a) Adultery, a criminal offence in several Latin American countries, is usually defined as sexual intercourse of a married woman with a man other than her husband. Single acts of sexual intercourse performed by married men outside marriage are not a criminal offence. Men can only be accused of concubinage, which is defined as the keeping of a woman other than the man's wife (therefore an element of continuousness is essential), if one of the following circumstances is present: i) Public scandal; ii) abandonment of the wife; iii) the concubinage taking place in the marital residence (Criminal Codes (Cr. C) arts.: Argentina: 118; Chile: 375, 381; Honduras: 431-435; Haiti: 285-287; Panama: 301, 302; Dominican Republic: 337-339; Venezuela: 396, 397). In all these cases, the punishment of concubinage is lighter than that of adultery. For example, in Panama adultery is punished with 1 to 2 years imprisonment, and concubinage with 1 to 10 months. In Venezuela, adultery deserves from 6 months to 3 years imprisonment; concubinage, from 3 to 18 months. In the Dominican Republic, adultery is punished with 3 months to 2 years imprisonment; concubinage with a fine.

b) In all legal systems, killing another person is in principle a criminal offence, which is aggravated if it is committed by a person with certain family ties with the victim (husband, wife, children). In five countries, however, to murder a wife caught in extramarital intercourse is either an exonerable criminal offence or one whose punishment is mitigated instead of aggravated (Cr. C. arts.: Colombia: 382; Haiti: 269 (2), 271; Honduras: 7 No. 15; Paraguay: 21 No. 7; Venezuela: 423). In some countries the exoneration or extenuation of the punishment benefits other close relatives when the victim is a daughter, sister or grand-daughter caught in sexual intercourse outside marriage, even if she is single and adult (Cr. C. arts.: Colombia: 382; Ecuador: 27; Mexico: 311; Venezuela: 423).

c) In almost all Latin American countries killing a new-born baby (infanticide) with the purpose of concealing the birth and thus the mother's or the family's shame, is a different criminal offence than homicide and is punished with a lighter sentence. The family's and/or the mother's honor are valued highly enough as to decrease the potential protection of life that the punishment of homicide purports to provide. This lighter penalty benefits not only the mother who committed the crime but also relatives who may have committed the offence irrespective of the mother's feelings and desires (Cr. C arts.: Argentina: 81; Brazil: 123; Colombia: 369; Costa Rica: 113 No. 3; Chile: 394; Guatemala: 129; Ecuador: 453; Honduras: 408; Mexico: 327; Panama: 316; Paraguay: 347; Peru: 155; Uruguay: 313; Venezuela: 413).

d) Abortion is also a criminal offence in almost all Latin American legal systems. The fact that it is so considered means in principle that in the eyes of the law the personal interests of the woman weigh less than the life of the unborn child. However, in fourteen countries a lighter sentence is given to the person who provokes the abortion and to the woman on whom it is performed if the reason is to conceal the mother's shame (Cr. C. Arts.: Bolivia: 265; Colombia: 389; Costa Rica: 93 No. 4, 119 and 120; Ecuador: 444; El Salvador: 165; Honduras: 411; Mexico: 332; Panama: 330; Paraguay: 349 (2), 353; Uruguay: 328 No. 1; Venezuela: 436). Only in Uruguay does the law consider, as circumstances mitigating the punishment, the fact that abortion is performed when the pregnancy was the result of rape (Cr. C: 328 No. 2) or when the reason is the economic problems of the parents-to-be (the latter is a major reason for abortion in Latin America) (Cr. C: 328 No. 4). It is quite significant that in both cases the lack of the woman's consent to the abortion is irrelevant for regulating the amount of punishment. The woman is here treated as a passive object of the action and not as the victim of an assault to her physical integrity. Although the only moral justification for considering abortion a crime is the fact that it is an attempt against life, in Chile abortion is categorized not as a crime against life but as a crime against the family order and public morality.

e) The penalty for rape depends in many countries on who the victim is. Generally if it is committed against an "honest" woman, the penalty is heavier than if the victim is not an "honest" woman. Although the word "honest" is never defined by the different legal provisions, it can be inferred from them that it is related to the woman's sexual conduct, and that by "honest" woman it is understood one who performs sexual intercourse only within the legal bond of marriage. This means that the value being protected by the punishment is not only, and often not mainly, the woman's freedom but her "honor". Sometimes the penalty is also heavier if the victim is a married woman, which shows that in the gradation of the punishment the protection of the husband's honor may play a more important role than that of the woman (Cr. C. arts.: Argentina: 120; Brazil: 215; Colombia: 317 No. 1, 321; Mexico: 262; Paraguay: 315; Venezuela: 393) An example will suffice. In Paraguay, rape is punished with eight to twelve years imprisonment if the victim is less than eleven years old; with six to ten years if the victim is older than eleven but younger than sixteen; with four to eight years if the woman is married; with three to six years if the victim is single, chaste and has a good reputation; with one to three years if the victim is single, but not a virgin; and with three months to one year if the victim is a prostitute, whichever her age (Cr. C: 315).[2]

Labour Law.

It is not difficult to understand that a woman given such a place in society will not be well equipped to face the world as an independent human being. Although non-discrimination is the formal general rule in Latin American labour law provisions, one cannot fail to observe that this fact notwithstanding, women are bound to have a secondary, minor place in the labour market. We could roughly divide working women between 1) those who work out of sheer financial necessity, and 2) those who work — the economic motivations notwithstanding — because they wish to do so, (probably because they possess a higher level of education or a special talent that they want to exercise). The second group, although probably relieved to a large extent from domestic work due to their economic capability to hire domestic service, is particularly affected by the fact that the rule of woman's obediency to men does not apply only to marriage and the family, and therefore there are often insurmountable obstacles for women to achieve positions of command (CEPAL, 1983: 176). Women from the first group very seldom have encouraging or self-fulfilling work. By definition, being a woman frequently means to remain at home and thus to receive little or no education. It should be remembered that in Latin American countries, giving an education to children is sometimes impossible because of economic reasons and families give boys the preference, among other motives, because of the legal obligation of men to provide for their families. One example to illustrate the point: article 389 of the Peruvian Civil Code sets forth that the duty to give *alimenta* to a son will be prolongued in time if he is succesfully following a career. In the case of the daughter, she is entitled to be financially supported when she is single and is not in a situation to earn her living.

The lack of education, aggravated by the above mentioned stereotyped image of women, results in women often ending up with the menial jobs in which their subservience to others matches their subservience to men at home. (CEPAL, 1983: 166-179) Domestic service is the most suitable instance, as it covers the activities of almost one-third of the women who work (CEPAL, 1983: 106) and is performed mostly by women (In Chile, 93,58% of all domestic servants were women in 1970. See Alonso, Larraín y Saldías, 1978: 400). A CEPAL study describes "domestic work" in Latin America as "the lowest kind of work as regards occupational prestige, satisfaction and remuneration" (CEPAL, 1983: 107). It is usually a 24-hour work with half a day free every week and could be compared with servitude (See Rubbo and Taussig). In Chile in the 70's, the average salary of domestic servants was half that of the minimum legal salary of a "blue-collar" worker, and less than 50% of these domestic servants were registered in, and therefore could not receive benefits from, the social security system (Alonso, Larraín and Saldías, 1978: 400-407). For these reasons, then, paid work is usually unattractive for these women, especially if it is considered that having such a job will not mean that they will stop doing their housekeeping. Under such circumstances it cannot be expected that women will have time and energy to think and connect the two sharply separated spheres that constitute a working woman's life and to process their new experiences into fruitful results. This situation, consequently, annuls or greatly diminishes the beneficial influence that paid work could have for the development of the women who perform it.

The role legislation plays in this scene is not a positive one. Most Latin American labour laws distinguish men from women for the sole effect of establishing protective provisions for the latter. Frequently the foundation of these legal rules is found in the constitutions themselves, making it thus more difficult for amendment (Constitutions: Brazil: 158 (x); Costa Rica:

71; Ecuador: 62; El Salvador: 182; Honduras: 124 (7); Mexico 123 (A.II) and (XI); Nicaragua: 95 (8); Panama: 69; Peru: 46; Uruguay: 54; Venezuela: 93). One positive aspect of this legislation concerns the protection of pregnant women (maternity leaves, relief from heavy work), but this aspect is blunted in its effects by the fact that it does not apply in the areas in which a majority of Latin American women work, namely rural work and domestic service (Vargas, 1975 in CIM, 1982: 312, 313). The rest of the protective legislation refers to prohibitions for women to perform certain works in order to protect either their health or their morality (Night-work, work in mines). It is not possible to justify a legal system that does not attempt to regulate unhealthy or dangerous conditions in order to make them healthier or safer, but instead only forbids them for women. As to the legal protection of women's morals, one can only say that it gives further evidence of a system which treats women as incapable of taking care of themselves, placing them in the same legal category of minors and mentally handicapped. As a consequence of this legislation, which is a refutal of the general formulation of non-discrimination provided in those legal systems, employing women becomes an inconvenience for employers, making it harder for women to find work (CEPAL, 1983: 180). Legislation, thus, not only does not counteract the discrimination women suffer in the labour market due to the several factors mentioned above, but adds to it through the provisions just mentioned.

The feminist struggle in the legal area. How and where.

It is within such societies that Latin American women must carry out their struggle for equality of rights. The Latin American feminist movement began their endeavour by striving to acquire political rights, as a useful instrument for further conquests. Such political rights exist now in all countries of Latin America, Paraguay having been the last to grant women the right to vote and to be elected to public office in 1961. The effects of this conquest, however, have been abated by two factors. One is that in many countries of the American continent these rights have been suppressed for years, so it is really ironical to count as a conquest the fact that women have been granted them. The other is that political rights serve their purpose only when exercised in freedom and with a sound and independent spirit. However, in general, the place that women occupy in society is often decisive in preventing them from making independent and advantageous political decisions, because of lack of political education and of the tradition of obediency and servitude to men, which inclines them to accept man's authority, also in this area. The feminist struggle in most Latin American countries has not gone much further, as can be demonstrated by the legal evidence we have analysed. It has been said that a main reason for this lack of success is that Latin American women have not found a common denominator to join forces due to the sharp differences which exist between the social classes (Astelarra 1981: 57-59). We suggest that fighting for the suppression of legal inequalities in civil, criminal and labour law could be an objective of great interest to a significant number of women and thus could serve the purpose of uniting women in a common struggle. We would further suggest that this struggle should be carried out based upon the premise that all human beings are free and equal before the law, and not upon the intellectual capacity or moral virtues of women, arguments which Latin American feminists have been inclined to use in the past.

It is essential that the struggle for equality of rights for women be inserted in the general struggle for respect for, and enjoyment of, human rights. That will provide it with a force and legitimacy which would be difficult to ignore by those who have to be persuaded.

As to where the struggle should be carried out, we would like to point out that the international arena should not be forgotten. Aside from the United Nations, Latin American women have a regional forum to work for their objectives: the Organization of American States (OAS). The OAS has since 1928 an Inter-American Commission of Women (CIM), the first official, intergovernmental body specifically created to secure the civil and political rights of women, and since 1960, an Inter-American Commission on Human Rights (IACHR) whose principal task is to promote the observance and protection of human rights and to serve as a consultative organ of the Organization in these matters. With the entry into force of the American Convention on Human Rights, in July 1978, a third organ was created, the Inter-American Court of Human Rights (IA Court), as another body for the protection of such rights (American Convention, arts. 33 and 52 ff.).

The Inter-American Commission of Women has notorious short-comings, probably stemming from the fact that it is to a large extent a reflection of the policies acceptable to the governments, as it is formed of government representatives and not independent individuals. However, it has potentials that could be developed with the right approach on the part of feminist organizations, particularly those within countries organized on the basis of representative democracy. First, the feminist organizations might press at national levels to have a say in the election of the delegate to the CIM, and have a say in what the delegate will do when representing her government in it. This would give feminist organizations some power to influence the activities of the CIM and the ideological base which guides these activities. Second, a clear and firm stand by the delegates of democratic countries on the fact that women's rights are human rights and that they should be handled as such would open up avenues for them to fight for their promotion and defense already existing in the OAS.

The Inter-American Commission on Human Rights, departing from the policies of the OAS as an organization, has been working for more than twenty years to promote and defend human rights and in that period has developed mechanisms and instruments to investigate and make public human rights violations, having acquired a reputation of seriousness and objectivity that would certainly serve the interests of women. This Commission, for example, writes country reports in which a detailed account is given of the situation of human rights in the country concerned as a form of exercising supervision on the observance of the rights. Why not ask the Commission, and provide it with information to that effect, to start supervising in a separate chapter of its reports the observance of women's rights? It has to be remembered that both the Declaration of the Rights and Duties of Man (although its very name begins by discriminating), as well as the American Convention on Human Rights contain provisions which should constitute the legal basis for the feminist movement in the Americas. The right of equality before the law and the prohibition to discriminate on grounds of sexual difference are set forth in both instruments (Declaration, art. II; Convention, arts. 1 and 24), as the right to be considered a person having rights and obligations and enjoying basic civil rights is also included in them (Declaration, art. XVII; Convention, art. 3).

The American Convention on Human Rights, in force since July 1978, offers still other possibilities. The Convention created an Inter-American Court of Human Rights which has powers to give advice to the member-states of the OAS on the interpretation of the Convention or of other treaties concerning the protection of human rights in the American States[3]. This advice may be requested not only by the states but also by the organs listed in Chapter X of the OAS Charter, one of which is the Inter-American Commission of Women, as a specialized organization of the OAS. Many rights in the convention, and above all the general principle of non-discrimination, could be given a more concrete form by way of the exercise of this advisory competence of the Court, which in the relatively short time it has been functioning has demonstrated its willingness to interpret its powers extensively to serve better its task. Women's organizations in democratic countries could also lobby to get their governments to consult the Court regarding the compatibility of any of their domestic laws with international treaties on human rights, and the advice of the Court could be used as weighty justification either for government action to change discriminatory provisions or for feminist organizations' action against a government which was willing to ask for advice but not willing to follow it.

Concluding remarks.

As conclusions it would seem appropriate to stress some points. First, the preceding legal analysis, however brief and incomplete, shows that there is legal discrimination against women in Latin American domestic civil, criminal and labour laws. In them , the traditional role of women in the family is enhanced and the values of a patriarchal society are reinforced. In the scarce areas where legal equality does exist, such as political rights, this equality is blunted by the many legal inequalities which place the woman in a position of dependency and ignorance and incline them to regard themselves not as complete human beings but only as wives, daughters, sisters or mothers, whose paramount task has been for centuries to protect their families as they are, thus to preserve the *status quo*.

Second, it is important in the struggle for women's rights to fight for the domestic legal recognition of specific equalities of the sexes using as legal justification the international law of human rights. It could be safely stated that presently there exists, at an international level, a formal consensus on the principle of equality of the sexes in all spheres. This should be the legal foundation supporting the struggle.

Third, in this struggle all legal mechanisms available should be utilized, be they national or international, and advantage should be taken of all *fora*. This is a lesson taught by similar movements striving for equality in other problem areas (race, religion). The legal mechanisms and the various *fora* should be set in motion to give them their own dynamics and a proper direction for the accomplishment of the objectives women set about to achieve.

NOTES

1) The importance of *patria potestas* has been painfully realized by women forced into exile. Children may not leave their country without their fathers' authorization, and this has caused many sufferings to legally or *de facto* divorced Latin American women.

2) I owe this example to the keen interest in feminism of Waldo Fortin, who most generously helped me with the research in Latin American domestic legislations.

3) On September 24, 1982, the Court gave an advisory opinion on the meaning of the words "other treaties subject to the advisory jurisdiction of the Court", concluding that "the advisory jurisdiction of the Court can be exercised, in general, with regard to any provision dealing with the protection of human rights set forth in any international treaty applicable in the American States, regardless of whether it be bilateral or multilateral, whatever be the principal purpose of such a treaty, and whether or not non-Member States of the inter-American system are or have a right to become parties thereto," (IACourt, 1983: 28).

REFERENCES

American Convention on Human Rights, reproduced in OAS, *Handbook of Existing Rules Pertaining to Human Rights in the Inter-American System* (Updated to September 1983), OEA/Ser. L/V/II.60, doc. 28, 26 July 1983, GeneralSecretariat, OAS, Washington, 1983.

American Declaration of the Rights and Duties of Man, reproduced in *Handbook*.

Alonso, Pablo et al. 1978. "La Empleada de Casa Particular: Algunos Antecedentes", in Covarrubias, Paz and Franco, Rolando, *Chile: Mujer y Sociedad*, UNICEF, Santiago, pp. 399-422.

Astelarra, Judith. 1981. "El Feminismo como Concepción Teórica y Práctica Política", in *Cuadernos ESIN*, No. 1, Instituto para el Nuevo Chile, Rotterdam, pp. 43-60.

CEPAL (Comisión Económica para América Latina), 1983. *Five Studies on the Situation of Women in Latin America*, United Nations, Santiago, Chile.

CIM (Comisión Interamericana de Mujeres), 1982. *Estudio Comparativo de la Legislación de los Países Americanos respecto a la Mujer*, Serie Estudios No. 7, Washington, Secretaría General, OEA.

Código Civil de la República Argentina, con reforma de la Ley 17.711, Ed: Luis A. Estivill, Buenos Aires, 1971.

Código Civil (Brazil), Carteira Forense, Konfino, Tomo I, Rio de Janeiro, 1973.

Código Civil (Chile), Séptima Edición, Editorial Jurídica de Chile, Edición Oficial al 31-VIII-76, aprobada por Decreto 1937 (Justicia), de 29-XI-76,

Santiago, 1977.
Código Civil (El Salvador), Constitución y Códigos de la República del Salvador. Recopilación efectuada por el Ministerio de Justicia, San Salvador, 1967.
Código Civil para el Distrito y Territorios Federales (Mexico), 330. Edición, Editorial Parrúa, S.A., México, 1972.
Código Civil de la República de Panamá. Anotado y concordado por J. Fábrega P. y Cecilio Castillero, Editorial Jurídica Panameña, 1973.
Código Civil (Perú), con notas por Jorge E. Castañeda, Lima, 1955.
Código Civil Venezolano, Dr. Armando Hernández Bretón, 2a. edición, Editorial La Torre, Caracas, 1961.
Código Penal de la República Argentina, Lajouane Editores, Buenos Aires, 1972.
Código Penal, Legislaçao Brasileira, Ediçao Saraiva, 9a. ediçao, 1972.
Código Penal y Código de Procedimiento Penal (Colombia). Con notas, concordancias, jurisprudencia de la Corte Suprema y normas legales complementarias por Jorge Ortega Torres, 16a. Edición Actualizada, Editorial TEMIS, Bogotá, 1978.
Código Penal y Leyes Conexas (Costa Rica). Nueva Edición. Revisada y preparada por el Lic. Atilio Vicenzi, Lib., Impr. y Litografía Lehmann, S.A., Costa Rica, 1975.
Código Penal para el Distrito y territorios federales (México), Vigésimo primera Edición, Mexico, 1972.
Código de Familia (Bolivia), Editorial Los Amigos del Libro, La Paz — Cochabamba, 1972.
Constitución de Chile, Editorial Júridica de Chile, Colecciôn Textos Legales No. 78, Santiago, 1981, pp. 45-137.
Inter-American Court of Human Rights, *Annual Report*, 1983, OEA:/Ser. L/V/III/9, doc. 13, September 3, 1983, OAS, General Secretariat, Washington, 1983.
Levine, Andrew. 1980. "Human Rights and Freedom", in Alan S. Rosenbaum (ed), *The Philosophy of Human Rights: International Perspectives*, Studies in Human Rights, No. 1. London, Aldwych Press. pp. 137-149.
Mattelart, Michele. 1975. "1975. Chile: The Feminine Side of the *Coup* or When Bourgeois Women take to the Streets", in *NACLA's Latin America and Empire Report*, IX (Sept. 1975), pp. 14-25.
Peaslee, *Constitutions of Nations*. 1970. Revised Third Edition, The Hague, Martinus Nijhoff, Volume IV, First and Second Parts.

Revolución, Latijns-Amerika Bulletin/Lente 1978, No. 25: "El Podor Femenino. De Mobilisatie van de vrouwen tegen het socialisme in Chili".

Rubbo, Anna and Taussig, Michael, n.d. *Up off their knees: Servanthood in South West Colombia, Women's International Resource Exchange Service, New York.*

Vargas Delaunoy, Inés, "Formación, Empleo, y Seguridad Social de la Mujer en América Latina y el Carribe", in Paredes, Querubina et al, *Participación de la Mujer en el Desarrollo de América Latina y el Caribe*, UNICEF, Santiago, 1975. Quoted in *CIM* 1982.

RACISM IN EVERYDAY EXPERIENCES OF BLACK WOMEN

Philomena Essed

Introduction

This paper presents a new approach to racism. It analyzes its systematic manifestations in everyday life from the point of view of those who experience racism. The study is based on data gathered in intensive interviews with black women in the Netherlands, and provides a summary of variations of three main forms of racism. After a discussion of feminist issues like the relation between sexism and racism in the experience of black women, an introduction to the semiotics of everyday racism is given by analyzing the problem of the interpretation of implicit discrimination in concrete social situations. The analysis of interpretation strategies opens new perspectives in the sociology and social psychology of interracial/ethnic relations and the meaning of racism. Black women are not presented as "victims", but as alert individuals who develop socially sensitive mechanisms as a form of expertise for the understanding of white attitudes and white behavior.

In the period after the Second World War, immigrants and migrant workers from various racial and ethnic backgrounds came to enrich Dutch society. The main groups came from (former) Dutch Colonies like Indonesia, Surinam, and the Dutch Antilles, and from Mediterranean countries (Italy, Spain, Yugoslavia, Greece and, later, from Turkey and Morocco). Together with political exiles of several nationalities (e.g. Chile, Bolivia, Ethiopia, Vietnam) they make up the Dutch ethnic 'minority' population. Well-known far across the national borders for their so-called hospitality, the Dutch had the opportunity to prove themselves worthy of that label. They failed the test. Racism is a fast growing national problem, especially for those who experience it.

Unfortunately, there is still very little academic research about racism in the Netherlands (see e.g. Bovenkerk 1978, Redmond 1980, van den Berg

& Reinsch 1983, van Donselaar & van Praag 1983, van Dijk 1983, 1984). Against the background of studies of racism in the United States and Great Britain, this paper presents a largely ignored, and therefore 'new' perspective on the understanding of racism: a systematic analysis of racism from an experiential point of view.

Interdisciplinary framework

My theoretical framework is fundamentally interdisciplinary, and draws upon work in micro-sociology, social psychology and women studies. Starting from a symbolic interactionist point of view, I define racism as a group interactional problem (Blumer 1958). Racism results from a specific kind of group conflict. We can only speak of racism when a racial/ethnic group is in the position of *power* and potentially uses its power and resourses to define and treat other racial/ethnic groups as inherently alien, and biologically or culturally inferior. This means that the concept of power is a constituent dimension of racism (Jones 1972, Wilson 1973). Power differences on the macro-level, that is, the hierarchical stratification of society and the oppressed position of racial/ethnic groups, are confirmed and reproduced on the micro-level of everyday interaction (see also Cicourcel 1981, Collins 1981). As a consequence the practice of racism is for black people part of their everyday experiences (Dummett 1973, Dworkin & Dworkin 1976, Levin & Levin 1982, Littlewood & Lipsedge 1982, Manning & Ohri 1982, Satow 1982). Therefore, in order to understand racism, it is relevant to analyze black people's daily experiences with white people and the way racism is defined within that context. For that purpose I introduce the concept *Everyday Racism*. Everyday racism refers to the way in which black people experience and understand racism.

The concept of 'experience' and the interpretation of experiences relate the micro-sociology of everyday racism to social psychological aspects. Everyday experiences are differentiated according to various everyday situations (home, work, school, and so on). For each situation and with respect to different actors, such as white neighbors, colleagues, teachers and fellow students, I explore the subjective experiences of black women. In their contacts with whites, black women are not dealt with as individuals, but as members of the 'other' group. As a consequence, black women's interpretation and evaluation of their personal experiences with white people are largely determined by their cognitions about their own social position as well as the cognitions they attribute to whites in order to understand racist behavior.

Women studies: black and white

This study of black women takes place against the background of recent developments in the field of women studies, and specifically studies about women of color. White feminist studies have been criticized for their underlying ethnocentrism (or 'whitecentrism') and for their implicit or open racism (see e.g. Rich 1979, and her contribution in this volume, Hooks 1981, Joseph 1981, Essed 1982, Bourne 1983, Frye 1983). Since the early seventies, the field of studies of women of color has grown steadily.[1] Although it is generally recognized that black women experience double, and in most cases even triple oppression — racism, sexism, and classism — (Davis 1981, Joseph 1981, Carby 1982), the specific meaning of racism in the lives of black women has not yet been systematically explored. White (women)'s racism and (black and white) men's sexism almost succeeded in making the black woman invisible (see also Jackson 1973). Here, I present black women's experiences and perspectives as a valuable and important source for the understanding of racism. This implies that scientific research has a good deal to learn from so-called ordinary women's experiences (Reinharz 1983). It relates women studies to Heider's original meaning of common-sense (social) psychology (1958) and to micro-sociology (Rogers 1983).

The problem

The main problem of this paper is: what specific signals and acts from white people are recognized as forms of racism in everyday experiences? Black people are regularly confronted with open and, due to the fact that racism is officially condemned, very often with implicit expressions of racism. This leads to serious *interpretation problems* in everyday contacts with whites. Therefore, an important corollary to the first problem is: what interpretation strategies are used in order to detect implicit discrimination? Black people have to deal with this crucial question systematically and almost daily.

The importance of an analysis of implicit and subtle forms of racism in daily interaction has been stressed before (see e.g. Pettigrew 1971, Cicourel 1982). But only few attempts have been made to establish an inventory of these acts of racism (see e.g. Rowe 1977, Hall 1982). Nor has there been any systematic analysis of interpretation processes used by ordinary people in the understanding of everyday (implicit) racism.

Method

These problems will be discussed with the help of data collected in preliminary research, consisting of interviews with fourteen Surinamese women in Amsterdam (the Netherlands) and nine Afro-American women in Berkeley-Oakland, California. For the purpose of this paper, only the experiences of Surinamese women are dealth with. The women were all in their twenties. Some of them had lived almost all their lives in the Netherlands, others only a few years. Most had received little education. Half of the group worked as nurse's aides in homes for the aged and for permanently sick people. A few women attended university or had just finished their studies. By using the so-called snowball system (Rubin 1976) a small and selective group was composed. I collected a range of accounts (Harré & Secord 1972) by non-directive interviewing. These were recorded on audio tape and transcribed in detail. As the research had an explorative character, I tried to make explicit, by comparison of several accounts, the subject's own categories of thought and action (Sjoberg & Nett 1968, Plummer 1983, Reinharz 1983).

Everyday racism

The women experience racism in numerous situations. Since we live in a racist society, racism occurs at all social levels and in contacts with ordinary Dutch people. In concrete situations racism always means that the acting white person reconfirms that s/he belongs to the powerful (white) group, and that s/he feels free to reject the black woman or treat her in an unfavorable way. The women gave a wide range of examples of everyday racism, which I categorized in three main forms:

1. To *define* or *treat* blacks as *inferior*,
2. to *create* social or spatial *distance* toward blacks.
3. to *practice* social or physical *aggression* toward blacks.

These main forms will be referred to below as ascribed inferiority, distance creation, and aggression, respectively, and will be illustrated with a few examples selected from specific situations.

A. House hunting

1. In the newspaper a woman reads advertisements saying: "No foreigners".

2. An employee at the department of housing keeps repeating every week when a Surinamese woman applies and asks whether an apartment is already available: "why don't you take one of those apartments in the Bijlmer (Amsterdam suburb)? You could move in right away. I mean, you people like to huddle together, don't you?".
3. A woman makes an appointment with a private housing agency by phone. On arriving there for further arrangements, the female employee she spoke with denies that she had her on the phone. The Surinamese woman explains the event as follows: "Maybe because I speak Dutch so fluently, one would not notice that I am a Surinamese woman when having me on the phone. But there were two gentlemen and only one woman at the agency, so I could not have been mistaken. I thought: I guess I understand what is actually going on here. I had never experienced this before. I knew about discrimination, but this .... no, really! I thought: just imagine what a judas she is. I could not understand that a person could be such a hypocrite".

In all three cases we recognize the principle of *distance creation*, either by avoiding any contact (case 1), by creating spatial distance (case 2) or by refusing certain association, such as supplying service (case 3). From the language used by the employee in the second case, we can infer *ascribed inferiority*. It would have sounded less humiliating to speak about people who like to live in the same neighborhood, apart from the fact that the suggestion itself is a prejudice. The third case can be evaluated as an instance of social *aggression*: the Surinamese woman presents the act of the white woman as intentional deception ("Such a hypocrite, she is a judas"), which can be understood as social harassment.

The above examples make clear that the three main forms of racism should not be seen as mutually exclusive. In concrete situations specific cases of the different main forms may be present simultaneously within one act (overlap), as is illustrated by the second and third case (distance creation/ ascribed inferiority and distance creation/aggression respectively).

B. Contacts with neighbors

1. One woman explains: "Their faces tell me that they don't want blacks in their streets".

2. A white man rings at his Surinamese neighbor's. Her youngest son opens the door. Without further comment, the man walks through the house, straight into the woman's bedroom. She just awakes from an afternoon nap and looks right into the man's face. On this event she remarks: "A Surinamese person would never have done such a thing. And I never enter their bedroom either, when I visit these downstairs neighbors".
3. A woman explains about her downstairs neighbor: "She used to harass us frequently, by complaining all the time about trivialities, like for instance: 'there is a leak somewhere', or, 'I hear strange noises, I'm sure it comes from your floor'. The Surinamese woman interprets this sort of behavior as follows: "This Dutch neighbor thinks: they are only Surinamese. So why should I care? I knock on their door and just complain whenever I feel like".

In the first example we find *distance creation*. The second case is an illustration of *ascribed inferiority*, which shows in the disrespectful and undecent way the woman is treated. Social *aggression* and ascribed inferiority can both be inferred from the third case. The specific cases (2,3) of the principle of ascribed inferiority may be qualified as rather typical. Also in other situations white people ignore manners when dealing with black people.

C. Work

At work (I refer here to Surinamese nurse's aides) the women experience various forms of racism. Let us look first at contacts with clients and patients.

1. White clients or patients often refuse to be served by a black: "Go away, I don't want a black nurse", or
2. "You can leave. I don't need assistance today".
3. A white senior woman has three nurses on night duty. They are all black. While she normally goes to bed at seven o'clock, she sits and waits long enough to have the one with the least dark skin color pass by. Then she asks: "Would you mind taking me to my bedroom?"
4. Black nurses are sometimes seen as maid-servants. When urged to put on her shoes, a white patient replies to the Surinamese nurse: "That is your job. That is what you are hired for".

Cases 1, 2 and 3 are clearly examples of distance creation. They differ, however, in the way this is acted out. The examples show how the same message is given openly (case 1) and implicitly (case 2 and 3). The third case also appears to have been planned strategically. In the fourth case we notice on the one hand social distance creation through ascribed inferiority (the white master gives orders to the black servant). On the other hand it appears that distance creation on the social level is facilitated by proximity on the spatial level (come near me and fasten my shoes).

With respect to contacts with white colleagues, Surinamese nurse's aides explain:

1. "Every time nurse D. had night duty with me, she pretended to be ill and did not show up".
2. "When I was not so long in the Netherlands yet, it used to take me a while before I was able to understand what my colleagues really meant, when they said something to me. They thought that it was because I was stupid. But I wonder how they would have felt if they were in Surinam and I would speak to them in Surinamese."
3. "At the coffee break, all coloreds join at one table. Sometimes we hear whites making remarks about this. They think that we do this out of political reasons. But I don't have such things in my mind at all. I just like to sit next to a friend."

Only one woman could tell from experiences as a black superior. She served as an advisor for white beginning nurse's aides.

4. "The students did not accept me. They refused to work with me. They kept hanging around in the kitchen or stayed in the bathroom while I attended a room full of patients waiting for their morning shower".
5. "One morning, I worked with one of the students. Instead of awakening the patient with: 'Good morning, how are you today?', he started a conversation like: 'What do you think of all those Surinamese people in our country, these days?' The patient of course replied what she had on her mind: 'I think these people should return to where they came from'. This student really did that on purpose. The students could be very blatant".

From some of the above cases distance creation can be inferred (cases 1,4,5). The third case sheds another light upon the principle of distance creation. Whites apparently find it unproblematic to keep blacks at a distance on their own terms. When blacks themselves choose to keep apart from whites this becomes problematic for the latter. Examples of ascribed inferiority and aggression can be found in case 2 and 5 respectively. Also, the fifth case is an example of strategically planned racist behaviour. Not wishing (or daring) to verbalize the racist idea that he does not want to work with a black nurse himself, the student uses one of the patients so as to keep himself free of the blame of being racist.

In their contacts with the head of the department, the women may experience racism as follows:

1. "The head nurse did not trust Surinamese nurses. She put us under extra control, by double checking whether we had done our work properly".
2. "I was in my second year and was allowed to give the patients their medicine. But the head nurse did not want me to do that. She believed I could not bear responsibility. But she wanted a white assistent, who was only in her first year and had not learned yet how to work with medicine to take over from me".

These examples show different dimensions of the principle of ascribed inferiority. In the first case the Surinamese woman's work ethos is questioned. In case 2 her abilities are denied.

D. School

In contacts with white fellow students Surinamese find:

1. "It suprised them that I got such high grades. From their conversations I could gather that they did not like that. They did not expect much from Surinamese students".
2. "In discussions it looked like I was not present. They totally ignored me".
3. "In a group discussion a white student said very racist things. It was clear that she considered us no more than a pile of shit. Another Surinamese student and I were very angry. The teacher did not know what to say. And then the other white students suggested to stop the conversation in order to avoid a fight".

Because black students are defined as intellectually inferior, fellow students do not appreciate evidence to the contrary (case 1). Social distance creation by seclusion shows from case 2. Social inferiority and social aggression can be inferred from the third case.
Similar kinds of racism are experienced from white teachers:

1. One woman explained that her teacher gave her too low grades for her Dutch. Even when she compared her work with that of another white student and could show that she deserved better, the teacher refused to change the grade.
2. At one of her oral exams a Surinamese student is confronted with racist remarks from a member of the committee. "she said things like: 'Why are all these foreigners here, they are stupid, and so on'. In trying to object against these remarks the Surinamese student is threatened with a low grade.
3. As part of her program a Surinamese student delivered a paper. She had worked hard on it, because she did not succeed on that specific task previously. But: "the teacher tore up the paper right before my eyes. He said that he was sure I had not written it by myself. At that moment I did not know what to do. There was nobody to turn to. So I wrote another paper".

A fundamental difference between racist students and racist teachers is that the latter have institutional power, which may have serious consequences for the students. The racist notion of ascribed inferiority may be translated into low grades or delay in the study schedule due to having to re-write a paper. Teachers can abuse their position of authority to keep black students from functioning adequately at school. This may cause the student to leave school, wasting study years and trying another school where it appears that racism is a problem there, also. Such effects were all found in my investigation.

Because of space limitations I do not elaborate on forms of racism in other situations. (For details, see Essed 1984). It may be concluded, however, that everyday racism is very often expressed *verbally*, as it also becomes diffused among the white majority by way of everyday conversation (van Dijk 1984). Without taking notice of the fact that the black woman might be within hearing distance, negative remarks and various kinds of prejudice are formulated, discussed and exchanged. If black women object, they will as a rule get answers like: "Of course we did not mean you. You are different from others".

Racism and Sexism

Experiences of black women make very good examples to illustrate how different kinds of oppression mutually stimulate or reflect each other (Kinloch 1979, Carby 1982). In relation to *white men* it can often be quite difficult or even impossible to differentiate between sexist and racist motivations behind certain acts. Take for instance the following event, presented by one of the interviewees, Linda:.

1. I went to a disco with my girlfriend.
2. On entering, the doorman says: "It is allright for you to visit our place, but don't bring black men with you".
3. Then I said to my friend: "Let us go away. I don't like it when he says such a thing to me".
4. But she said: "We have already paid, so why don't we go inside all the same?"
5. I said: "Okay". And in we went.
6. She and I started to dance together, but suddenly a white man put his hands on my buttock.
7. I was absolutely furious.
8. I called him names and said: "How dare you presume that you can grab any black woman that crosses your path!".
9. I was really angry and wanted to go home immediately.
10. The thing was that I already felt fucked up with this doorman.
11. It meant that my boyfriend would not have been welcome.
12. If he is not welcome I don't want to go there either.
13. Because they just discriminate. (Essed 1984)

A closer look at this interview fragment illuminates several aspects. In first instance it looks like the doorman's racism was not directly aimed against Linda. As we notice, only black men were explicitly mentioned as not being welcome (line 2). Linda, though, identifies with the men from her group (line 12) and experiences therefore what I describe as *inferential racism*. Inferential racism refers to any racist act committed against another group member which as a consequence of identification is interpreted as a racist act against yourself. Because of the doorman's racist remark Linda would have liked to leave right away (line 3, 10). Persuaded to stay, she then experiences sexism (sexual harassment) and racism (note line 8, where she refers to 'any *black* woman' and not to 'any woman') within the same act. Now we can return to the doorman and re-evaluate his previous statement. It becomes clear that he must have acted out of sexism (two women alone) and racism (black women are even more than white women seen as sexually available).

Sexism and racism mutually reinforce each other in the above example. Note that racism and sexism can also be each other's mirror image. The racism black women experience from *white women* can resemble the sexism white women themselves experience from men. This will be illustrated with an example taken from a school situation. Both against women as a group and against blacks as a group, the stereotype exists that they are less intelligent than 'men' and 'whites' respectively (Levin & Levin 1982). Carla, one of the interviewees remembered from university classes:

1. Take for instance that we were to write a joint paper.
2. The white girls would only ask each other to participate in their group, and I would remain alone.
3. Nobody would ask me. I had to look for a place by myself.
4. In the group, my contribution was always minimal,
5. because they thought they had more to say than I did.
6. My suggestions were evaluated longer before they were accepted for the paper.

If we substitute 'white girls' in line 2 for 'boys', the example could have been taken from a study of sexism and supposed female intellectual inferiority (see e.g. Hall 1982). The same holds true for examples where (white female) teachers and supervisors abused their institutional position to undervalue black women's achievements (Rowe 1977). The above example also shows that seclusion (distance creation) can be achieved without openly stating that the black woman is unwanted (line 2,3). Effective seclusion did not imply active (positive) acts. As we noticed from previous examples also, passive (negative) acts like ignoring, withholding support or attention, and overlooking, are frequently used forms of implicit discrimination.

Interpretation strategies in the detection of implicit discrimination

We have already found that everyday racism is acted out in numerous verbal and non-verbal ways. These acts presume, explicitly or implicitly, that black women are inferior, that their presence is not wanted, or only acceptable under certain conditions, and that they may be treated aggressively because they belong to an 'inferior' group. Superficially, one might find such acts of daily racism only 'trivial' or 'small' humiliations (see also Rowe 1977 in this respect). Yet, the same patterns of prejudice and discrimination reoccur in contacts with different whites and in different situations. This creates for black women the opportunity, or rather the necessity, to observe and analyze white behavior systematically and to try out new interpretations and evaluations in future situations. Black women gradually develop expertise in the interpretation and evaluation of white behavior. This holds specifically true for the numerous — or as one of the Afro-American women describes it: "thousand ways" in which whites practice racism. On the basis of previous experiences with racism, black women are quickly able to recognize racism in new situations, even when the racist intention remains implicit.

An interpretation fragment

With an example I will illustrate what an interpretation fragment looks like. I quote a Surinamese woman, Olga, who tells about her everyday shopping.

1. Especially in shops I experience discrimination.
2. I enter the 'Etos' (a well-know drugstore) and this male attendant literally follows me.
3. And I can tell you, on purpose I bought a plastic bag at the 'Bijenkorf' (big department store). That bag is so transparent, that one would notice immediately if I would steal anything. Whenever I have another bag with me, I intentionally put it at the cashier's.
4. So I say to this man: "The way you stand there looking and looking at me makes it unpleasant for me to do my shopping".
5. I say: "You are observing mé, but the Dútch are the ones who steal!"
6. His reply: "It is not true that I only look at you".
7. Then I said: "Well, I'm sorry but I do feel it that way".
8. The next day, I intentionally went back to buy some sandwich bags. I wanted to find out whether he would do it again, whether he would really control me.
9. I leave the sandwich bags on the shelf and go to the perfume department.
10. He approaches me saying: "Can you find what you are looking for?"
11. I answer: "I am just looking".
12. Yet, he keeps following me.
13. At that point I told him: "Don't expect that you will ever see me again in your shop".
14. I said: "Why did you specifically notice me when I entered?"
15. "I mean, so many women came in with me at the same time. But you do not follow them".
16. Says he: "Sure, but the Surinamese ..."

17. I say: "What about the Surinamese! You look at me while the others are stealing!"
18. And this did not only happen at 'Etos', you know. That is also why I don't go to 'Simon de Wit' (Supermarket) anymore.
19. And in entering 'Blokker' (store for household articles) I always leave my shopping bag at the cashier's.
20. Also in the 'Hema' (department store) for instance, I always take care never to walk around with three or four friends.
21. Because I know that they are watching us (Essed 1984).

Although it is rather artificial to isolate this fragment from the rest of the interview, and so from Olga's other experiences, this will do for the purpose of highlighting some aspects of the interpretation process. It is important to stress that we are not analyzing interpretation processes Olga went through in the original situation in the shop. Rather, we analyze the ad hoc interpretation as presented in the interview situation. Yet, we may assume that the interpretation strategies expressed in the interview are similar to those used to detect and evaluate the racist acts in the original situation (see also Marsh et al 1978). For reasons of space, I ignore the functional strategies imbedded in the interview situation itself — for instance explanations or persuasive arguments aimed at the interview partner. Also, I do not discuss the semiotic dimensions of these interpretation processes, as studied from a social psychological point of view (attribution theory, cognitive dissonance theory, and intergroup theory and the role of social cognition). For the moment I focus on the *sources of information*, the kinds of knowledge, Olga uses for the interpretation and evaluation of her experience:

1. *Own previous experiences.*

In an implicit way, Olga tells us that she is quite familiar with the experience of being followed suspiciously in shops, and with the racist prejudice that Surinamese people steal. That is why she as a rule takes precautions which she thinks will have a preventive effect: she does not want to be accused wrongly. We notice that she has bought a transparent shopping bag for that purpose, that in case she shops with another bag, she will always leave it at the cashier's desk (line 3), and that she avoids being seen in a group (line 20).

2. *Comparison with other people.*

Olga compares the man's behavior toward her, with his behavior toward white women. She has noticed that the shop attendant specifically watched only her, while several other women entered the shop simultaneously with her. Note how she indicates this observation. She does not say explicitly: I saw so many other *white* women enter. Instead she first refers to the 'other women' (line 15) and then contrasts 'the others' against 'the Surinamese' (line 17). Note also in line 5 where she explicitly explains: "The Dutch are the ones who steal".

3. *Own observations*

In first instance the attendant denies that he was observing Olga specifically (line 6). Olga suspects, though, that he actually discriminates her but that he does not want to admit this openly. To check whether her suspicion (read: preliminary evaluation) is right, she creates a try-out situation, a real life experiment, so to say. The scheme is that she returns the next day to observe the white man's behavior more closely. We already know the story. He follows her again and Olga has noticed that he only follows her, and not the other women who had entered the shop (line 8-15).

Apart form having verified her previous judgement *indirectly* (to put the situation to the test and to re-eavaluate) her suspicion is proven right also *directly*. In the discussion following her protest against his discriminative behavior the attendant (accidently?) states: "But the Surinamese ..." (line 16). This is a direct confession.

4. *Comparison with similar situations.*

Olga indicates that the experience in 'Etos' should not be seen as typical for that drugstore or for that specific white shop attendant. Apparently, she experienced something similar in a supermarket. This we can infer from her explanation that for that reason ("that is why", line 18), she does not go to 'Simon de Wit', that supermarket, again.

5. *General beliefs, opinions, expectations and other cognitions*

Olga tells that she knows that in general Surinamese people are watched (line 21). For that reason she also takes precautions at 'Blokker', even though as far as we can judge from the fragment she has not been bothered (yet!) at that shop. But because she apparently believes (knows) that racism is not a characteristic of a specific white person, she has no illusions about the shop attendants at 'Blokker' either ("And in entering Blokker ...", line 19).

It appears from the data that other women also use these information sources. Sources not mentioned in this fragment, but which are found with respect to the interpretation of other events are given below and illustrated with examples: (Essed 1984)

6. *Comparison with other (black people).*
    1. A Surinamese nurse's aide was questioned impertinently by the head nurse. She indicated that she evaluated this behavior as racist by explaining: "All other black girls, no matter whether you were Surinamese or Moroccan, were also questioned about their private matters by this same head nurse".
    2. A Surinamese student left the university, because she was afraid a specific teacher would flunk her at the examination. Previously he had always given her very low grades and very negative criticism. The woman interpreted his behavior as follows: "He presumed that Surinamese students could not do better in Dutch language than Dutch students could. And for him it even did not matter if you have lived in the Netherlands all your life". In order to argue that her fear of being flunked was real and that the teacher acted out of racist motivations, the woman refers to experiences of other black women: "Later it appeared, so I heard from others, that he really discriminated against blacks. Two other Surinamese girls, who, unlike me, had continued, were nearly flunked. He would have flunked them, hadn't they filed a complaint. They went to the school director and made a case out of it".
7. *Opinions of others*
    1. A first example can be found in the above quotation where the Surinamese student refers to others ("I heard from others that he really discriminated", which stands for: 'others acknowledged that my evaluation was right').
    2. The case where a white senior woman deliberately chose the nurse with the lightest skin color to bring her to bed (see under: 'C. Work'), apart from this direct observation, was also verified as being a form of racism by the argument: "Every one at the department knew that she was like this". The Surinamese interviewee verifies this argument further by adding: Whenever I was on night duty with two white nurses they would propose to me: 'Why don't you take mrs. V. to her bedroom tonight, so we can hear her screaming'.

On the basis of my preliminary inquiry we may conclude that the detection of implicit discrimination is a complex process in which comparisons, tests, re-evaluations, systematic observations, and the like are involved.

Arguments that claim that blacks would be 'over-sensitive' can now be qualified as misguided. From the black women's experiences we should rather infer that they develop *socially sensitive mechanisms* tuned to analyze and classify white behavior in general, and acts of racism, implicit and explicit, in particular.

NOTE

1) As studies of women of color are not widely known yet, I suggest the following publications for introductory readings: *The United States*: Cade 1970, Lerner 1970, Ladner 1972, Reid 1972, Epstein 1973, Jackson 1973, Smith 1977, Noble 1978, M. Wallace 1978, Bell e.a. 1979, the Combahee River Collective 1979, Mirandé & Enriquez 1979, Sterling 1979, Christian 1980, P. Wallace 1980, Davis 1981, Hooks 1981, Joseph & Lewis 1981, Moraga & Anzaldúa 1981, Hull, Scott & Smith 1982, Baraka & Baraka 1983, Smith 1983. *Great Britain*: James 1975, Sharpe 1976 (Chapter VIII: "Black Girls in Britain"), Wilson 1978, Amos & Parmar 1981, Carby 1982, Fuller 1982, Parmar 1982, Bourne 1983, Phizacklea 1983. *The Netherlands*: Nalbantoglu 1981, Lenders & van de Rhoer 1983, Essed 1984.

REFERENCES

Amos, Valerie & Parmar, Pratibha. 1981. "Resistances and Responses: the Experiences of Black Girls in Britain". Angela McRobbie & Trishna McCabe (eds). *Feminism for Girls*. London: Routledge & Kegan Paul. 129-148.
Baraka, Amiri & Baraka, Amina. 1983. *Confirmation. An Anthology of African American Women*. New York: Quill.
Bell, Roseannn P.; Parker, Bettye J.; Guy-Sheftall, Beverly (eds). 1979. *Sturdy Black Bridges: Visions of Black Women in Literature*. New York: Anchor.
Berg, Harry van den & Reinsch, Peter. 1983. *Racisme in schoolboeken* (Racism in School-Books). Amsterdam: SUA.
Blumer, H. 1958. "Race Prejudice as a Sense of Group Position". *Pacific Sociological Review 1*. 3-7.
Bourne, Jenny. 1983. "Towards an Anti-Racist Feminism". *Race & Class, XXV, 1*: 1-22.
Bovenkerk, Frank (ed). 1978. *Omdat ze anders zijn. Patronen van rasdiscriminatie in Nederland* (Because They Are Different. Patterns of Race Discrimination in the Netherlands). Meppel: Boom. (1979).
Cade, Toni (ed). 1970. *The Black Woman. An Anthology*. New York: New

American Library.
Carby, Hazel V. 1982. "White Woman Listen! Black Feminism and the Boundaries of Sisterhood". Centre for Contemporary Cultural Studies. *The Empire Strikes Back.* London: Hutchinson. 212-235.
Christian, Barbara T. 1980. *Teaching Guide to Accompany Black Foremothers: Three Lives,* by Dorothy Sterling. Old Westbury, New York: The Feminist Press.
Cicourel, Aaron V. 1981. "Notes on the Integration of Micro- and Macro-Levels of Analysis". K. Knorr-Cetina & A.V. Cicourel (eds). *Advances in Social Theory and Methodology. Toward an Integration of Micro- and Macro-Sociologies.* Boston: Routledge & Kegan Paul. 51-80.
Cicourel, Aaron V. 1982. "Living in Two Cultures: the Everyday World of Migrant Workers". Unesco. *Living in Two Cultures.* Paris: Unesco. 17-65.
Collins, Randall. 1981. "Micro-Translation as a Theory-Building Strategy". K. Knorr-Cetina & A.V. Cicourel (eds): 81-108.
The Combahee River Collective. 1979. "A Black Feminist Statement". Zillah Einstein (ed). *Capitalist Patriarchy and the Case for Socialist Feminism.* New York: Monthly Review Press. 362-372.
Davis, Angela. 1981. *Women, Race and Class.* London: The Women's Press. (1982).
Dijk, Teun A. van. 1983. *Minderheden in de Media* (Minorities in the Media). Amsterdam: SUA.
-----. 1984. *Prejudice in Discourse. An Analysis of Ethnic Prejudice in Cognition and Conversation.* Amsterdam: Benjamins.
Donselaar, Jaap van & Praag, Carlo van. 1983. *Stemmen op de Centrumpartij* (To Vote on the Centrum Party). Leiden: Centrum voor Onderzoek naar Maatschappelijke Tegenstellingen.
Dummett, Ann. 1973. *A Portrait of English Racism.* Harmondsworth: Penguin.
Dworkin, Anthony Gary & Dworkin, Rosalind J. 1976. *The Minority Report.* New York: Holt, Rinehart & Winston. (1982).
Epstein, Cynthia Fuchs. 1973. "Positive Effects of the Multiple Negative: Explaining the Success of Black Professional Women". Joan Huber (ed). *Changing Women in a Changing Society.* Chicago: University of Chicago Press. 150-173.
Essed, Philomena. 1982. "Racisme en feminisme" (Racism and Feminism). *Socialistiese Feministiese Teksten 7.* 9-40.
-----. 1984. *Alledaags racisme.* (Everyday Racism). Amsterdam: Sara.

Frye, Marilyn. 1983. "On Being White: Thinking Toward a Feminist Understanding of Race and Race Supremacy". *The Politics of Reality: Essays in Feminist Theory*. New York: Crossing Press. 110-127.
Fuller, Mary. 1982. "Young, Female and Black". Ernest Cashmore & Barry Troyna (eds). *Black Youth in Crisis*. London: Allen & Unwin. 87-99.
Hall, Roberta M. 1982. "The Classroom Climate: a Chilly One for Women?". *Project on the Status and Education of Women*. Washington: Association of American Colleges.
Harré, R. & Secord, P.F. 1972. *The Explanation of Social Behaviour*. Oxford: Basil Blackwell. (1979).
Heider, F. 1958. *The Psychology of Interpersonal Relations*. New York: Wiley.
Hooks, Bell. 1981. *Ain't I a Woman. Black Women and Feminism*. Boston, Mass.: South End Press.
Hull, Gloria. T.; Scott, Patricia Bell; Smith, Barbara (eds). 1982. *But Some of Us Are Brave. Black Women Studies*. Old Westbury, New York: The Feminist Press.
Jackson, Jacquelyne Johnson. 1973. "Black Women in a Racist Society". Charles Willie, Bernard Kramer & Bertram Brown (eds). *Racism and Mental Health*. Pittsburgh: University of Pittsburgh Press. 185-268.
James, Selma. 1975. *Sex, Race and Class*. Bristol: Falling Wall Press.
Jones, James M. 1972. *Prejudice and Racism*. Mass.: Addison-Wesley.
Joseph, Gloria. T. 1981. "The Incompatible Menage à Trois: Marxism, Feminism, and Racism". Lydia Sargent (ed). *Women and Revolution*. London: Pluto. 91-107.
Joseph, Gloria L. & Lewis, Jill. 1981. *Common Differences: Conflicts in Black and White Feminist Perspectives*.
Kinloch, Graham C. 1979. *The Sociology of Minority Group Relations*. Englewood Cliffs, N.J.: Prentice-Hall.
Ladner, Joyce A. 1972. *Tommorrow's Tommorow*. The Black Woman. New York: Anchor.
Lenders, Maria & Rhoer, Marjolein van de. 1983. *Mijn God hoe ga ik doen? (My God, what am I going to do?)* Amsterdam: SUA.
Lerner, Gerda. 1972. *Black Women in White America. A Documentary History*. New York: Vintage. (1973).
Levin, Jack & Levin, William. 1982. *The Functions of Discrimination and Prejudice*. 2nd. ed. New York: Harper & Row.
Littlewood, Roland & Lipsedge, Maurice. 1982. *Aliens and alienists*. Har-

mondsworth: Penguin.
Manning, Basil & Ohri, Ashok. 1982. "Racism — the Response of Community Work". Ashok Ohri, Basil Manning & Paul Curno (eds). *Community Work and Racism*. London: Routledge & Kegan Paul. 3-13.
Marsh, Peter; Rosser, Elisabeth & Harré, Rom. 1978. *The Rules of Disorder*. London: Routledge & Kegan Paul.
Mirandé, Alfredo & Enríquez, Evangelina. 1979. *La Chicana*. Chicago: University of Chicago Press. (1981).
Moraga, Cherríe & Anzaldúa Gloria, (eds). 1981. *This Bridge Called My Back. Writings of Radical Women of Color*. Watertown, Mass.: Persephone.
Nalbantoglu, Papatya. 1981. *Aysel en de anderen. Turkse vrouwen in Nederland* (Aysel and the others. Turkish Women in the Netherlands). Amsterdam: Sara.
Noble, Jeanne. 1978. *Beautiful, Also, Are the Souls of My Black Sisters*. Englewood Cliffs, N.J.: Prentice-Hall.
Parmar, Pratibha. 1982. "Gender, Race and Class: Asian Women in Resistance". Centre for Contemporary Cultural Studies. *The Empire Strikes Back. Race and Racism in 70s Britain*. London: Hutchinson. 236-275.
Pettigrew, Thomas F. 1971. *Racially Separate or Together?* New York: McGraw-Hill.
Phizacklea, Annie (ed). 1983. *One Way Ticket. Migration and Female Labour*. London: Routledge & Kegan Paul.
Plummer, Ken. 1983. *Documents of Life. An Introduction to the Problems and Literature of a Humanistic Method*. London: Allen & Unwin.
Redmond, Roline. 1980. *Zwarte mensen in kinderboeken*. (Black People in Children's Books). Den Haag: Nederlands Bibliotheek en Lektuur Centrum.
Reid, Inez Smith. 1972. *"Together" Black women*. New York: The Third Press. (1975).
Reinharz, Shulamit. 1983. "Experiential Analysis: A Contribution to Feminist Research". Gloria Bowles & Renate Duelli Klein (eds). *Theories of Women's Studies*. London: Routledge & Kegan Paul. 162-191.
Rich, Adrienne. 1979. "Disloyal to Civilization: Feminism, Racism and Gynephobia". *Chrysalis* 7. 9-27.
Rogers, Mary F. 1983. *Sociology, Ethnomethodology, and Experience. A Phenomenological Critique*. Cambridge: Cambridge University Press.
Rowe, Mary P. "The Saturns Rings Phenomenon: Micro-Inequities and

Unequal Opportunity in the American Economy". Patricia Bourne & Velma Parners (eds). *Proceedings*. Santa Cruz: University of California. (Preprint).

Rubin, Lillian Breslow, 1976. *Worlds of Pain*. New York: Basic Books.

Satow, Antoinette. 1982. "Racism Awareness Training: Training to Make a Difference". Ashok Ohri, Basil Manning & Paul. Curno (eds). *Community Work and Racism*. London: Routledge & Kegan Paul. 34-42.

Sharpe, Sue. 1976. *Just like a Girl. How Girls Learn to Be a Woman*. Harmondsworth: Penguin. (1981).

Sjoberg, Gideon & Nett, Roger. 1968. *A Methodology for Social Research*. New York: Harper & Row.

Smith, Barbara. 1977. *Toward a Black Feminist Criticism*. New York: Out & Out Books. (1980).

-----. (ed). 1983. *Home Girls. A Black Feminist Anthology*. New York: Kitchen Table: Women of Color Press.

Sterling, Dorothy. 1979. *Black Foremothers: Three Lives*. Old Westbury, New York: The Feminist Press.

Wallace, Michele. 1978. *Black Macho & the Myth of the Superwoman*. London: John Calder. (1979).

Wallace, Phyllis A. 1980. *Black Women in the Labor Force*. Cambridge, Mass.: MIT Press.

Wilson, Amrit. 1978. *Finding a Voice. Asian Women in Britain*. London: Virago.

Wilson, William. J. 1973. *Power, Racism, and Privilege*. New York: Free Press. (1976).

"I FOUND GOD IN MYSELF AND I LOVED HER/ I LOVED HER FIERCELY": MORE THOUGHTS ON THE WORK OF BLACK WOMEN ARTISTS.

Michelle Cliff

The thesis of this essay[1] is that there is a complex, essential and energized connection between the visual art of Afro-Americans, specifically but not exclusively the art of Afro-American women, and the visual art of those African nations from which the slaves, the ancestors of these artists, were taken. This connection is part of a larger connection, which includes philosophy, language, music, theology. Unless the cultural relationship between African and Afro-American artists is understood, one cannot fully appreciate the tradition of Afro-American works of art. The relationship between the art created by Afro-American women and the art of Africa is manifested by specific aspects of the work: the images created, the symbolic meaning of these images, materials used, form, color, standards of beauty, three-dimensionality, usefulness. The relationship is also manifested in larger questions and responses: the idea of art, the purpose of art, what constitutes a work of art, for what art is made, art as an expression of certain theological principles, certain philosophical principles. What follows is an exploration into this connection, touching on a few of these links; to investigate them all would require at least one book.

To begin any examination into the culture of Afro-Americans, one must begin at the point of origin — with groups such as the Yoruba, the Kongo, the Fon, the Ewe, the Mande, the Ejagham. When the slave-traders descended on the west coast of Africa in the sixteenth century and thereafter (the Atlantic slave trade lasted from about 1550 to 1850), they were met by inhabitants of urbanized, advanced, and sophisticated civilizations. Of all the nation/groups listed above, only the Ejagham were or could be considered a rural people; and they had organized towns as well as rural settlements. All the other nation/groups were highly and complexly urbanized, and had been urbanized since what Europeans call the Dark Ages. In his essay "The Atlantic Slave Trade", the Black Marxist philosopher C.L.R. James quotes the following from Claude Lévi-Strauss (1980: 236)

> The contribution of Africa is more complex, but also more obscure, for it is only at a recent period that we have begun to suspect the importance of its role as a cultural melting pot of the ancient world: a place where all influences have merged to take new forms or to remain in reserve, but always transformed into new shapes.

He concludes that even the Egyptian civilization is "intelligible only as a common product of Asia and Africa."

This was pre-European Africa, what James called "a territory of peace and happy civilisation." (p. 236). I stress this fact about Africa because even though it is not a new discovery, the reverse racist image with which we are all familiar persists — that is, that the slaves came from a place which was wild and primitive, and that they themselves knew little better than to submit to slavery by white men. This includes the white assumption that Africans would respond only to back-breaking labor, and when they slacked off, to physical punishment of another sort — whether whipping, rape, branding, or mutilation. That image of Africa and Africans simply was a lie — but this lie was necessary to underwrite another lie; that slavery was justifiable, and that the slavery of Black Africans was not the crime against humanity that enslaving white Europeans would have been. This false image of Black Africans as uncivilized is related to another historical lie, part of a complex network of distortion and amnesia, that is, that once in the New World, forcibly separated from their families and mixed with other linguistic and cultural groups, the Africans lost whatever civilization they had and reverted to primitivism and simplicity. There was a loss, of course, but it was by no means total — perhaps *change* or *tranformation* would be better words than loss for what happened to the Africans. James has written: that the slaves came from large areas of West Africa, in which "dozens upon dozens of distinct peoples lived," with their own languages, cultures, religions (p. 243-244). The slave only brought the content of his mind, his memory since he could not bring material objects.

> He valued that which his previous life had taught him to value; he feared that which he had feared in Africa; his very motions were those of his people and he passed all of this on to his children [...]. All Africans were slaves, slaves were supposed to act in a specific way. But what was this way? There was no model to follow, only one to build. (p. 244).

The Africans who came to the New World were from nations of advanced peoples, and their civilizations — the cultural and ethical standards they represented, the values they embraced — were not things which slid over the side during the Middle Passage, nor did the content of their minds and memories disappear in the barracoons, nor in the seasoning stations, on the auction block, in the quarters. As James points out, it was not easy to hold on to one's language, older social customs, culture, and something was lost, but aspects of other African nations were added, and individual talents and experience were remembered. Picture if you will, not the enchained and naked bodies of men and women locked in a forced march, a common, and true image of Africans in slavery in America, but rather try to imagine millions of individuals — both words deserve equivalent stress: millions and individuals. There *were* millions: estimates range from the conservative figure of 15.000.000 slaves landing in the New World to 50.000.000 (James 1950: 239); numbers are not known for those who died en route — from illness and overcrowding, suicide, or as the casualties of the many slave-led revolts on shipboard — nor for those who were born into slavery in the New World. Imagine millions of individuals who were singers, traders, artists, agricultural workers, soldiers, diplomats, historians, inventors, cartographers, bankers, sculptors, dancers, educators, textile designers, potters, ceramicists, ironwork artists, blacksmiths, ceremonial drummers, composers, midwives, physicians, astronomers, architects. Imagine these people, the true wealth of their minds and memories, and you will have a more accurate idea of what the system of enslavement entailed. Think of the wealth these individuals brought with them, and you will have a sense of how America was constructed. Think also of the culture which existed within slavery — which the slaves built from the store of their minds and memories, contact with other Africans, and the new world in which they found themselves. Newspapers published. Music composed and performed. Works of art created. Acts of healing. Acts of bravery. Thread spun and cloth woven. Political organizations. Children educated. Stories remembered and reconstructed. History recorded. A new language — made from African languages and the language of the slavemasters — devised. A faith — extraordinary in its belief in justice and the right to freedom — made from African religion and philosophy and the Judeo-Christian Bible — built. This belief in the right to freedom and the possibilities of justice is most important; to quote James again:

> It must be said that the slave community itself was the heart of the abolitionist movement. This is a claim that must seem extraordinarily outrageous to those who think of abolitionism as a movement which required organiza-

tions, [...]. Yet the centre of activity of abolitionism lay in the movement of the slaves for their own liberation. (1980: 253)

It has, of course, been said that there was a docility on the part of the African slaves, which led to the conclusion that slavery suited them, that their spirits had been broken; they had no anger, no sense of nation or self left. This is another white lie that needs to be put to rest. It *has* been put to rest — by Frederick Douglass, Sojourner Truth, Harriet Tubman, W.E.B. DuBois, Lorraine Hansberry, and C.L.R. James, among others[2] — but it keeps rising up, so I must place it in its grave once again, fixing a bag of salt on top to forbid its resurrection. There was a massive opposition on the part of Africans to their situation in slavery, which, had they not carried with them memories of the juridical creations and philosophical doctrines of Africa, as Lévi-Strauss has named them, might not have been possible. Learning to read in secret, on penalty of blinding or death; organized, armed insurrection, on shipboard and on land; domestic subterfuge in the great house; freed slaves working to buy freedom for friends or relatives or friends of friends; artisan slaves — that is, those who worked at crafts on the plantations, like smithing, coopering, etc. — hiring themselves out to raise money to buy freedom, for themselves, for others; slaves somehow raising money to fund revolutionary organizations; slaves stealing from the slavemasters to supply revolutionary organizations; freepeople like Mammy Pleasant sending thousands of dollars to people like John Brown, to fund his raid on Harper's Ferry;[3] women inducing abortion and committing infanticide to deny the slaveowner another commodity, another means of production; women feigning pregnancy to deceive the slavemaster and so refuse enforced breeding; women caring for the children of other women, when the mothers were sold away; a massive, synchronized movement of escape, led by, among others, the brilliant visionary and strategist Harriet Tubman — all of these things, and more, should prove that there was no acquiescence on the part of slaves with regard to their enforced servitude.

Perhaps the great American tragedy — because this is a tragic nation — is that whites were able to use the talents of slaves to construct a powerful country, without taking also, or even respecting, the systems of thought and ethics and society that lay in the minds and memories of the Africans.

To further understand how history has been stood on its head by white American racism, consider, for example, the spiritual; the musical mode whites tended to regard as an expression of the slaves lulling themselves into submission, passively waiting for the sweet by-and-by, captured by the other-world promise of Christianity. Songs like "Go Down, Moses," "Steal Away," and "Swing Low, Sweet Chariot" were songs of insurrection and encoded communication, as well as mourning, but never were they songs of acquiescence. And they had African content — both in music and words, as stated by Maud Cuney Hare in *Negro Musicians and their Music* (1967), who speaks of the African origins of "Swing Low, Sweet Chariot": a tribe near the Victoria Falls in Rhodesia, had a custom in the old days, that when one of their own chiefs was about to die, he was put in a canoe, together with food and the trappings that marked his rank. Meanwhile the tribe would sing its chant of farewell:

> The legend is that on one occasion the king was seen to rise in his canoe at the very brink of the falls and enter a chariot that, descending from the mists, bore him aloft. The incident gave rise to the words 'Swing Low, Sweet Chariot,' and the song, brought to America by African slaves long ago, became anglicized and modified by their Christian faith. (p. 22).

The song existed in several versions. In a private conversation, the Black political scientist and writer, Gloria I. Joseph has suggested that one version might have been "Swing Low, Sweet Harriet," in reference to Harriet Tubman and the Underground Railroad, just as "Go Down, Moses" and "Steal Away" were directly connected to Harriet Tubman, as she alerted slaves to get on board. In Africa, references to "home" in songs like "Swing Low, Sweet Chariot" may have meant an afterlife; in America these references were as likely to mean a return to Africa, or to freedom.

In her important article, "Black Women and Music" (1983), Irene V. Jackson describes the relationship to music of both women in Africa and slavewomen in the New World. In both African cultures and New World slave communities, women had charge of and responsibility for many forms of song — particularly songs to accompany rites of passage; for example, women composed and sang all mourning songs and funeral laments, to ease the journey of the dying and the dead and to provide catharsis for the mourners.

In my research and reading for this essay I have been struck again and again by the fact that in African cultures, in Afro-American slave communities, and in post-emancipation Afro-American communities the role of the older woman has been as a leader, as someone given enormous respect because of her understanding of matters of life and death, her wisdom of insight and experience. With regard to this task of women, particularly older women, in easing pain and loss, Maud Cuney Hare tells the following story of the appearance of "Swing Low, Sweet Chariot" in the slave South (1967: 22). It is said it arose from an incident which happened to a woman sold from a Mississippi to a Tennessee plantation. Rather than to be separated from her child, she was about to drown herself and the child...

> ...When she was prevented by an old Negro woman, who exclaimed, "Wait, let de Chariot of De Lord swing low, and let me take the Lord's scroll and read it to you." The heartbroken woman became consoled and was reconciled to the parting. The song became known with the passing on of the story.

Jackson (1983) makes the connection between the spiritual and the Blues and Gospel, of which Afro-American women have been the primary practioners. The link between African funeral songs and the Blues and Gospel was the spiritual — what W.E.B. DuBois called the sorrow songs. The continuum includes Harriet Tubman singing "Steal Away" as she entered the quarters to gather slaves for the journey north, Billie Holliday singing "Strange Fruit," as the signature tune in her nightclub act, an insurrectionist lament performed for the most part in front of white audiences, and Nina Simone singing "Mississippi Goddam" during the Civil Rights movement and "To Be Young, Gifted, and Black" after the death of Lorraine Hansberry. All three singers, it must be noted, paid a price for their actions and their voices.[4] The knowledge that they might pay some price did not stem their song.

II

> The Yoruba assess everything aesthetically — from the taste and color of a yam to the qualities of a dye, to the dress and deportment of a woman or a man. An entry in one of the earliest dictionaries of their language ... was *amewa*, literally "knower of beauty," "connoisseur," one who looks for the manifestation of pure artistry. Beauty is seen in the mean ... Moreover, the Yoruba appreciate freshness and improvisation ... in the arts (Thompson, 1983: 5).

If everything is assessed aesthetically — from a yam to a riff to a poem to a dance to a greeting — then aesthetics, style, can be known to all people, because beauty can be found in all things. Art and the recognition of artistry are accessible and not reserved for an elite. Created and understood by the milliner, the quiltmaker, the gardener, the poet. Found in the audience. In the dress of a Sunday morning congregation. The movement and voice of the Amen Corner. Ntozake Shange has a poem called "We Dress Up"; it is about the sense of style of Afro-American people and their tradition of dressing for occasions, for treating ceremonies and gatherings with respect — for me this stands for never taking life for granted; making it, in fact, special.

Spoonbread and Strawberry Wine (1978) is a cookbook/family history by two Afro-American sisters, blood sisters, Norma Jean and Carole Darden. It is a book filled with a demand for style — and the importance of display and beauty in individual behavior and deportment, as well as in food and drink. The artistry demanded in display — of the individual, of her/his surroundings — is not hollow; with it goes the expectations of an individual's striving — hard work, education, decency, caring belief in the excellence of one's self, one's own. Life is never taken for granted. No automatic advantage is expected. What is expected is adversity, but the struggle against adversity can be won in a beautiful way.

I have other responses to the description of the Yoruba by Robert Farris Thompson — particularly with regard to Afro-Americans. It is impossible to read of the Yoruban appreciation of "freshness and improvisation" and not think of Blues, Jazz, Be-bop. Or not be reminded of Lévi-Strauss's statement that Africans took the influences of other parts of the ancient world and always transformed them into new shapes.

The Yoruba comprised Africa's largest population group; in addition, the Yoruba had enormous influence and effect on other African peoples, both in Africa and the New World. The society of the Yoruba was comprised of self-sufficient city-states, each one characterized by "artistic and poetic richness" (Thompson 1983: 5). Much of this cultural richness was created to honor the Yoruba religion. The pantheon of Yoruban deities included the following:

        Eshu — individuality and change
        Ogún — iron
        Ifá — divination
        Yemoja/Yemayá — seas
        Oshun — sweetwater, love, giving
        Oshoosi — hunting
        Obaluaiye — disease and earth
        Nana Bukúu — mother of Obaluaiye, witchcraft
        Shàngó — thunder
        Obatálá — creativity

Overarching this collection of gods and goddesses is Olorun — God Almighty — ruler of the skies — neither male nor female. Olorun's gift to men and women is *àshe*, the power-to-make-things-happen, the energy of Olorun made accessible to men and women to be used by them according to their own judgment.

Àshe is found in certain animals: the python (ere); the gaboon viper (oka olushere); the earthworm (ekolo); the white snail (lakoshe); and the woodpecker (akoko). *Àshe* is also present in iron, blood, and semen, and in certain trees.

In his description of how an object may represent *àshe* — that is, an object created by human being — Thompson speaks of a ceramic bowl made to honor Shàngó, the thunder God: zigzag patterns, Y-shaped representations, rectangular emblems:

> Time and again the story of the descent of God's *àshe*, in multiple forms, in multiple avatars, is suggested ideographically upon this important vessel. To the right and to the left of the central square emblem appear chiefly scepters, underscoring the essential nobility of the persons who embody and comprehend the power-to-make-things-happen. The three concentric circles suggest three stones, the kind Yoruba women use to support their cooking vessels, meaning that adherence to the moral sanctions of Earth supports us all, safeguarding the equilibrium of the country and its people. (p. 6)

The bowl Thompson describes not only represents *àshe*; it embodies *àshe* — "A thing of a work of art that has *àshe* trancends ordinary questions about its make-up and confinements; it is divine force incarnate" (p. 21). Perhaps the most striking thing about African philosophy is its emphasis on the symbolic. Every being, action, thing possesses or is given a symbolic meaning. An example of this is in the three cooking stones to which Thompson refers above — how these become, given an African interpretation, not just plain domestic tools, but things which stand for something else as well; in this case the balance of the world brought about by moral behavior.

That said, I would like to turn to a discussion of the sources and power of what I consider one of the major works of art created in America in its history: the Second Bible Quilt of Harriet Powers. It is a work immersed in symbolism, and in the power-to-make-things-happen. The actual translation of *àshe* (while essentially untranslatable) is "so be it," "let it happen." For me, Harriet Powers's quilt is a work which expresses such a prophetic, magical vision. It is a vision which is expressed through the imagery of the Judeo-Christian Bible, but also through African symbolism. And, like the ceramic bowl made to honor Shàngó, Powers's quilt is charged by spirituality and the passion of the gods she honors with her work.

III

> The Negro has not been christianized as extensively as is generally believed. The great masses are still standing before their pagan altars and calling old gods by a new name.
> — Zora Neale Hurston, "The Sanctified Church"

Harriet Powers was born in 1837 in Georgia; her parents had been brought from Africa as slaves. In her article on Powers's pictorial quilts — of which two survive — Marie Jeane Adams observes that the generation of Harriet Powers's parents came to the New World at a time when slaves were primarily taken from the Kongo and Angola (Adams 1979). They would have brought the traditions of those regions of Africa with them and would have been one source of African knowlege for their daughter. It should also be noted, however, that the new slaves, once in America, would have been mixed with populations of slaves whose origins were other places and cultures of Africa, at a time when the various African traditions, and African languages, were being combined into Afro-American tradition and language. It is important to keep this in mind — this condition of social and cultural mixture — when trying to understand how Mrs. Powers learned the method by which she represents her vision, and the sources of the various elements in her vision, because it is a syncretic work, her quilt, taking from a variety of cultures.

Her method of working is appliqué — a distinctly African invention — found in two particular cultures, both of whom were plundered by the slave-traders: the Fon of Dahomey and the Ejagham of southwestern Cameroon and southeastern Nigeria. Among the Fon, appliquéd textiles were ceremonial cloths, used as costume, festival decorations, and wall hangings, which festooned the palaces of Dahomeyan kings, as well as other religious and secular spaces. Powers's Second Bible Quilt was also a ceremonial cloth, made to decorate a wall at Atlanta University, a Black college, on commission from a group of Black women who were wives of professors of the school.

The themes of the Dahomeyan wall hangings were historical and religious, representing symbolically scenes of events that had taken place in the kingdom; one such hanging at first glance appears nothing more than a display of animals, but the animals are in fact symbolic representations of several Dahomeyan kings.

Marie Jeane Adams comments on the similarity between the style of Mrs. Powers and the style of the textile designers of the Fon: general approach to depiction, massive figures arranged at angles:

> The images are also placed roughly in rows. Both employ human figures, animals and objects as motifs which are repeated in simple form. Perhaps the most consistent formal similarity is the degree of curvature in shaping of the images. Both obviously aim for a comprehensive view of their subject. (p. 25)

The Ejagham also employed the method of appliqué in their textile designs. Whereas the Fon used symbols to represent certain personages, the Ejagham are particularly noted for the existence of a complex system of ideographic writing — *nsibidi*; among the practitioners of *nsibidi* were members of secret societies, separate societies of women and separate societies of men. In fact, the tracing of *nsibidi* symbols on appliquéd cloth is a female practice.

> It was the Ejagham female who was traditionally considered the original bearer of civilizing gifts. Ejagham women also engaged in ... aristic matters. Their "fatting houses" (*nkim*) were centers for the arts, where women were taught, by tutors of their own sex, body-painting, coiffure, singing, dancing, ordinary and ceremonial cooking, and, especially, the art of *nsibidi* writing in several media, including ... appliqué. (Thompson 1983: 34)

From another source, an Efik woman, is the following:

> It used to be thought that the girls just went into the fatting-house to' get fat and idle away their time. This is nonsense ... during the time of their seclusion they were given serious instruction in dancing, comb-making, care of children, embroidery, and many other things, including how to make symbolic appliquéd cloths (*mbufari*). (p. 34)

The power of women was well respected among the Ejagham. One version of the origin of the ideographic system is that mermaids emerged to present the gift of *nsibidi* to the Ejagham. The system of ideographs ranges from signs for ordinary objects, signs representing qualities that exist in human relationships (love, hatred, disunity, unity), signs that represent human activities, etc. There are in addition a whole series of signs, called the "dark signs" — colored in dark shades — that represented things of "danger and extremity" (p. 245). In some cultures, to which the ideographic system of the Ejagham had spread, *nsibidi* was entirely a woman's art and method of communication for initiates.

I am not saying that the symbols used by Harriet Powers in expressing her vision in the Second Bible Quilt are necessarily taken directly from the system of *nsibidi*, but I am saying that the idea of levels of meaning, the deeper levels of meaning known only by initiates, the decoration of a seemingly ordinary object with images of power, so that the ordinary object becomes endowed with this power, are things which her quilt holds in common with the *mbufari* of Ejagham women, as well as the ceramic Yoruban bowl discussed above.

Specifically, image by image, Harriet Powers's quilt contains symbols which occur in several African cultures. What follows is a diagram of the quilt according to Powers's own description, and a discussion of the quilt frame by frame.

It is my opinion that we should approach the quilts of Harriet Powers as the work of an artist both conscious of and in control of her images, and that the viewer needs to recognize that there is a plan to the construction of the work of art, in which the frames can be seen in relation to each other as well as separate scenes which convey messages.

The following two pages show the construction of the second bible quilt.

THE SECOND BIBLE QUILT

1. Job praying for his enemies. Jobs crosses. Jobs coffin.

2. The dark day of May 19, 1780. The seven stars were seen 12.N. in the day. The cattle all went to bed, chickens to roost and the trumpet was blown.

3. The serpent lifted up by Moses and women bringing their children to look upon it and be healed.

6. Jonah casted overboard of the ship and swallowed by a whale. Turtles.

7. God created two of every kind, Male and female.

8. The falling of the stars on Nov. 13, 1833. The people were frightened and thought that the end of time had come. God's hand staid the stars. The varmints rushed out of their beds.

11. Cold Thursday, 10. of Feb. 1985. A women frozen while at prayer. A man with a sack of meal frozen. Icicles formed from the breath of a mule. All blue birds killed. A man frozen at his jug of liquor.

12. The red light night of 1846. A man tolling the bell to notify the people of the wonder. Women, children, and fowls frightened but God's merciful hand caused no harm to them.

13. Rich people who were taught nothing of God. Bob Johnson and Kate Bell of Virginia. They told their parents to stop the clock at one and it would strike one and so it did. This was the signal that they entered everlasting punishment. The independent hog which ran 500 miles from Georgia to Virginia. Her name was Betts.

MORE THOUGHTS ON THE WORK OF BLACK WOMEN ARTISTS

OF HARRIET POWERS

4. Adam and Eve in the garden. Eve tempted by the serpent. Adam's rib by with which Eve was made. The sun and the moon. God's all-seeing eye and God's merciful hand.

5. John baptising Christ and the spirit of God descending and rested upon his shoulder like a dove.

9. Two of every kind of animals continued, camels, elephants, "gheraffs," lions, etc.

10. The angels of wrath and the seven vials. The blood of fornications. Seven headed beast and 10 horns which arose out of the water.

14. The creation of animals continues.

15. The crucifixion of Christ between the two thieves. The sun went into darkness. Mary and Martha weeping at his feet. The blood and water run from his right side.

Frame 1 represents the first Biblical illustration in the quilt — in which there are ten Biblical illustrations in all. In this frame, Mrs. Powers represents the story of Job. This first frame also introduces one of the themes of the quilt — the suffering of the righteous and their eventual deliverance by God. Job stands as an *exemplum* of this theme, as he was righteous, and subjected to suffering in order to test his faith in Yahweh. There is a clear parallel here to the position of Africans in slavery, and the moral test to which enforced servitude put them, as there is in many of the frames.

My eye was caught by the two crosses in the upper corners of the frame. By calling them "Jobs crosses" I presume Powers may have been referring to the two calamities which befell Job and which he had to bear: the loss of family and home, and the physical pain he was subjected to — again, the parallel with Africans in slavery is direct and clear. But that is only one level of the artist's meaning.

The crosses are, I think, meant to foreshadow the crosses in the last frame, which represent the final redemption of the crucifixion; and, further, to recognize a relationship between the passion of Job and the passion of Christ — one as a *type* for the other. The quilt, then, embodies a journey from suffering to redemption: beginning with Job and ending with Jesus. Why are there two crosses in the first frame and three in the final frame? I think the answer to that question is that the coffin in the first frame, balanced as it is by stars or suns at each of the four points, is meant to be a third cross, set off from the other two as Christ's cross is elevated in relation to the crosses of the thieves.

The form of the two crosses in the first frame is very significant; they are not the elongated Latin cross but the equilateral Greek cross, and this is, I think, a signal to another level of vision. (I should also mention that the Greek cross is a recurrent motif in Harriet Powers's First Bible Quilt.) The Greek cross is a symbol intrinsic to the philosophy of the Kongo people; it is a charged image, standing for their belief in life without end.

> This Kongo "sign of the cross" has nothing to do with the crucifixion of the Son of God, yet its meaning overlaps the Christian vision. Traditional Bakongo believed in a Supreme Deity, Nzambi Mpungu, and they had their own notions of the indestructibility of the soul. "[...]" The Kongo *yowa* cross [...] signifies the equally compelling vision of the circular motion of human souls about the circumference of its intersecting lines. The Kongo cross refers ... to the everlasting continuity of *all* righteous men and women. (Thompson 1983: 108)

That such a concept existed in Africa, and that its meaning was represented by a cross, tells us something about the acceptance by Afro-Americans of the concept represented by Christianity.

In some representations of the Kongo cross it is a simple Greek cross; in others it is a Greek cross with a disk at each of its four points. This more elaborate version of the Kongo cross is described as follows.

> Initiates read the cosmogram ... respecting its allusiveness. God is imagined at the top, the dead at the bottom, and water in between. The four disks at the point of the cross stand for the moments of the sun [i.e., the solstices and equinoxes], and the circumference of the cross the certainty of reincarnation: the especially righteous Kongo person will never be destroyed but will come back in the name or body of progeny, or in the form of an everlasting pool, waterfall, stone, or mountain. (Thompson 1983: 109)

The figure of Job's coffin, with its four points, star/sun disks at each point, fixed between the two Greek crosses, stands, I think, for this version of the Kongo cross. In fact, the message of the cosmogram is captured by the way in which Mrs. Powers has rendered the image. By fixing the four moments of the sun to each point of the coffin she has transformed what is commonly a symbol of the end of human life to a symbol of everlasting life, in which death, represented by the coffin, is but one stage.

You will note that the word *righteous* is used in each description of the Kongo cross and what it signifies; that is, the Kongo people believed in life everlasting, but only if the individual had earned it by living righteously. Mrs. Powers was concerned with the rewards given the righteous, and the punishment earned by those who were not, as the pivotal thirteenth square shows.

Thompson makes a point in his book *Flash of the Spirit* (1983) of describing the strong survival of Kongo culture and tradition in the New World: "Kongo civilization and art were not obliterated in the New World: they resurfaced in the coming together, here and there, of numerous slaves from Kongo and Angola" (p. 109). The parents of Harriet Powers were among these slaves. I stress this, because as Thompson states, only until relatively recently has it been acknowledged that there is a connection between the visual art of Africa and the visual art of Afro-America, and the symbols found in each.

The second frame of the quilt is the first representation of a calamitous event of nature; there are four such representations in the quilt. In this frame, Mrs. Powers depicts the dark day of May 19, 1780, a day, as Marie Jeane Adams points out, that was known as Black Friday, in New England, when the daytime sky turned dark from the effect of forest fires. People who witnessed the event were convinced the world was coming to an end (Adams 1979: 12). To highlight the calamitous nature of the event, a dark sign perhaps, and the fear that the time of judgment was due, Powers has used the seven stars and an angel's trumpet, symbols of the Book of Revelation. This book of the Bible has inspired several Afro-American artists — James Hampton, Minnie Evans, Sister Gertrude Morgan for example — in telling their visions. It is that book which contains — of all in the Bible — the most absolute statement of God's judgment, a statement captured through a complex variety of symbols, all balancing in the end justice and mercy with punishment and wrath. The energy which the Book of Revelation conveys is not unlike the *àshé* of the Yoruba — the final power-to-make-things-happen, and the work of the Afro-American artists I have mentioned all move from the realm of decorative art to pieces which the artist intends to be charged with the power of God.

All the natural events to which Powers refers in the quilt have to do with changes in the heavens and atmosphere; and I think, and will discuss further later, that there may be a consciousness of Shàngó, the thunder god who rules the heavens, in these choices. There can be no doubt as to her intentional choice of these events, especially given the fact that only one occurred in her adult lifetime. The others all occurred during the time of African enslavement.

Frame three of the Second Bible Quilt illustrates an event which occurred during the forty years in which the Children of Israel wandered in the desert. Moses is the central human figure. The Black anthropologist and novelist Zora Neale Hurston was fascinated by the figure of Moses. Hurston traced Moses's survival as an African figure through several of the cultures of the New World. She writes of him in the following extract from her chapter on the Voodoo gods in her book *Tell My Horse* (1938: 138-140):

> Damballah Ouedo is the supreme Mystere and his signature is the serpent. [...] This worship of Moses recalls the hard-to-explain fact that wherever the Negro is found, there are traditional tales of Moses and his supernatural powers that are not in the Bible, nor can they be found in any written life of Moses. The rod of Moses is said to have been ... serpent and hence came his great powers.

Hurston wrote a novel entitled, *Moses, Man of the Mountain*; in the preface to the novel she identifies Moses as a Dahomeyan deity specifically, whose temples, whether found in Africa or in the New World, are decorated with a living serpent, or the representation of a serpent (1939: 7-8).

Of all the events in the life of Moses, it is most interesting, and I think, significant, that Harriet Powers chose to depict Moses using his magic serpent as an instrument of healing. Among the Fon of Dahomey the good serpent Dā or Dan is a god, one who combines male and female aspects, whose province is the sky. His/her avatar is the rainbow serpent, a figure which also occurs under a different name in Kongo and Yoruba religions (Thompson 1983: 173-77). In Haiti the name for Dā or Dan is Damballah.

As with the Kongo crosses in the first frame, Mrs. Powers has included an African image in this frame, supplementing or combining African belief with her understanding of the Judeo-Christian Bible. Throughout the quilt the Biblical imagery can be noted for two things: a reference to the slavery of Africans in America and their eventual redemption through emancipation; the use of figures and events from the Bible that do not contradict African belief systems but complement them or reinforce elements of African belief. The Second Bible Quilt is an excellent example of how African belief systems mixed with the faith the slaves found in the New World. If we bear Hurston's discovery in mind, we realize that the slaves recognized Moses not only as the leader of the Israelites out of bondage, but also as an African god whom they remembered for his magical powers and by the presence of his avatar, the rainbow serpent.

The identification of Harriet Tubman as Moses because she was a leader of her people is one thing; Harriet Tubman as Moses, a magician taking power from African tradition, one who was guided by visions and dreams, is something else. Of this latter Tubman there is the following, taken from the biography/oral history of Tubman's life, compiled by Sarah Bradford (1974: 118-119). Just before she met Captain John Brown, she dreamt she saw a serpent in the bushes, whose head became that of an old man, gazing at her, and two other heads rose younger than he. The three looked at her so "wishful":

> This dream she had again and again, and could not interpret it; but when she met Captain Brown ... behold, he was the very image of the head she had seen. But still she could not make out what her dream signified, till the news came to her of the tragedy of Harper's Ferry, and then she knew the other two heads were his sons.

Like Tubman, John Brown has been identified in the Black imagination as a Mosaic figure in Afro-American history; an identification which is apparent in Harriet Tubman's dream. Moses in the wilderness, with his attribute/

avatar, the serpent.

The fourth frame in the Second Bible Quilt is Harriet Powers's depiction of the story of Adam and Eve in the Garden of Eden. Several of the figures in the frame have African content. The serpent does of course, on one level, refer to the snake who tempted Eve. But it may also, especially given the fact that it follows the frame depicting Moses and the rainbow serpent, refer to Dā or Dan, who coiled his body around the earth to create a globe. The snake's body is large and curved, for one thing, much larger than usual depictions of the snake in Eden; there is, in addition, no tree of knowledge, a common attribute of the snake, in Powers's frame. This frame depicts part of the story of creation; to see in it the creature believed to have shaped the earth is not far-fetched.

Particularly, this frame depicts the creation of the male and female of the human species. That is why I think the presence of the sun and moon have additional meaning. The highest deity of the Fon was Mawu-Lisa — the moon and the sun; the female and the male. Mawu, the female, represents gentleness and coolness; Lisa, the male, fire and strength. Their union represents a "Fon ideal" (Thompson 1983: 176). It is as if the figures of Adam and Eve, with their hands clasped, reflect this union of Mawu-Lisa; a possibility made more likely given the fact that the moon is visually related to the figure of Eve, whereas the sun is visually related to the figure of Adam.

The eye of God in the frame is an additional African detail. According to the Yoruba:

> "The gods have "inner" or "spiritual" eyes ... with which to see the world of heaven and "outside eyes" with which to view the world of men and women" (Thompson, 9).

In the frame, both the world of heaven and the world of men and women are illustrated and envisioned. When a human being becomes possessed of *àshe*, "the radiance of the eyes, the magnification of the gaze, reflects *àshe*, the brightness of the spirit."

Frame five shows the familiar story of the baptism of Christ by John the Baptist, and God's spirit descending in the form of a dove. Among the Yoruba, *iwa rere*, good character, also known as *coolness*, was the goal of human beings who wished to achieve a higher level of behavior and being. *Iwa rere* is, like *àshe*, a gift of Olorun, God Almighty, who is also called Lord of Character, *Olu Iwa*. Good character is found in the mind, which is represented by a bird. The bird in the mind, which stands for character, echoes the descent of Olorun's *àshe* to the earth, also in the form of a bird.

> Yoruba kings provide the highest link between the people, the ancestors, and the gods. Their relation to the creator is given in following ... "The king, as master of *àshe*, becomes the second of the gods." Birds, especially those connoting the *àshe* of "the mothers," those most powerful elderly women with a force capable of mystically annihilating the arrogant, the selfishly rich, or other targets deserving of punishment, are often depicted in bead embroidery ... at the top of the special crowns worn in Yoruba kings ... these feathered avatars ... protect ... the leader. (Thompson, 7-9)

The sixth frame on the quilt depicts the story of Jonah, echoing the story of Job told in the first frame.

Frame seven is Powers's first of three frames showing the creation of pairs of animals by God. These animal frames deserve closer examination for what the animal types may represent; they serve also as the most positive frames in the quilt, a relief from the themes of the other frames, they are evidence of God's power-to-make-things-happen, to create, in beauty.

The eighth frame is the second frame which depicts a natural cataclysm; the first of two which have to do with meteor showers. Here Powers depicts a Leonid meteor storm which took place on November 13, 1833, and lasted for eight hours. This particular meteor storm is listed in the *Encyclopedia Brittannica*, eleventh edition, as one of sixteen major meteor storms, from the year 902 to 1868. As with the "dark day" of May 19, the observers of the meteor storm were convinced the world was about to end.

Meteors, or shooting stars, have a certain significance in African tradition. Among the Kongo, shooting stars were believed to indicate spirits traveling across the sky. Among the Yoruba, meteors indicate the power of Shàngó, the thunder god, who is sometimes depicted as carrying two flaming meteorites on his head. Shàngó is particularly characterized by the Yoruba as the god of vengeance (Thompson, 85). Like the god of the Old Testament, of Jonah and Job and Moses, Shàngó is capable of both mercy and wrath; he is a god who carries his power and his vengeance through the heavens — his force embodied in thunder, lightning, meteors. The apparent conflict in Shàngó's personality — he is a god of justice, judgment, combining fury and tenderness — is spoken of in the following Yoruban hymn:

> Father, grant us the intelligence to avoid saying stupid things.
> Against the unforeseen, let us do things together.
> Swift king, appearing like the evening moon.
> His very gaze exalts a person.
> I have an assassin as a lover.
> Beads of wealth blaze upon his frame.

> Who opens wide his eyes.
> Leopard of the flaming eyes
> Fire, friend of the hearth.
> Leopard of the copper-flashing eyes
> Fire, friend of the hearth.
> Lord with flashing, metallic eyes,
> With which he terrifies all thieves. (Thompson, 56)

Within this frame I cannot help but notice the male figure Mrs. Powers has created — with her use of light and dark cloth, he seems as if he were split in half: "Shàngó splits the wall with his falling thunderbolt" (p. 85).

One final note about this frame: Shàngó's signature color is red, and both this frame and frame twelve, depicting the "red light night" use this color to great effect.

Frame nine continues the creation of the animals by God. In this frame it is notable that all the animals are African animals: elephants, giraffes, lions, camels.

Frame ten follows. The message of the Book of Revelation, with its promise of deliverance for the righteous, and unremitting punishment for those who follow the *beast* has been used, as I mentioned above, by other Black artists. In her song, "New World Coming," Nina Simone juxtaposes a political vision, a world of "peace, joy, and love," against the message of the Book of Revelation; the singer quotes some of the words of Revelation directly, as if the events of the book must first occur in order to make a new world, a transformed political order, possible. I believe Mrs. Powers's quilt carries a similar message.

While reading the Book of Revelation to find exactly which images Mrs. Powers has chosen, and perhaps why, I found the following:

> And the merchants of the earth weep and mourn ... since no one buys their cargo any more, cargo of gold, silver, jewels and pearls, fine linen, purple, silk and scarlet, all kinds of scented wood, all articles of ivory, all articles of costly wood, bronze, iron and marble, cinnamon, spice, incense, myrrh, frankincense, wine, oil, fine flour and wheat, cattle and sheep, horses and chariots, and slaves, that is, human souls. (18: 11-13)

This is one of the few places in the Bible where it is implied that slavery is an unjustifiable human condition. The building in this passage of commodities from gold and silver to "slaves ... human souls" suggest slavery as the extreme of materialism, and final proof of human worship of the *beast* rather than God.

This frame in the quilt contains, I think, a statement by Mrs. Powers of her judgment that the slaveholders are servants of the seven-headed beast and that they will be punished on the final day. The seven vials hold the seven final plagues which will befall the wicked; the angels and their trumpets will initiate this visitation of God's justice. And the symbol between the three angels, as it were connecting them — I am not certain but that it might represent a slender version of the Kongo cross, which would certainly fit with the message of the frame.

Mrs. Powers, in this frame and throughout the quilt, takes it upon herself to judge — like the Yoruban "mothers," with a "force capable of mystically annihilating the arrogant, the selfishly rich, or other targets deserving of punishment." The Bible warns its adherents to "judge not, lest ye be judged"; it is a very powerful commandment. But in African religions, the righteous person is given the responsibility to judge, and the responsibility to mete punishment. Mrs. Powers takes this responsibility throughout her work, certain in her belief that her judgment is a just one.

In frame eleven, the artist depicts another natural occurrence; the only one in the quilt occuring in her adult lifetime. And the only one which occurred after emancipation. This is interesting, especially since this is a frame in which the hand of God does not stay the forces of nature, and in which human beings die. I do not think this frame necessarily fits with the other frames showing natural calamities or upheavals. Perhaps its message is that punishment will come from God in any case; that jubilee, emancipation, did not free white slaveholders from accountability. The year 1895 is an important detail; by that year the system of segregation in the American South had been codified. The promises of Reconstruction had been rescinded. 1896 would see the Supreme Court uphold the cynically named and economically absurd "separate but equal" doctrine in their *Plessy vs. Ferguson* decision. Perhaps Harriet Powers's message contains the recognition that racism, the exploitation of Black people, by no means ended with emancipation, rather was redefined, reinstitutionalized, and that therefore God's wrath continues. But perhaps even God cannot alter the course of events for Afro-Americans. "A woman frozen while at prayer" is a telling image — and a disturbing one.

We are not sure, for one thing, whether the woman is meant to be white or Black.

There may also be an element of autobiography in this frame in the quilt. In the years after emancipation, while poor, Mrs. Powers and her husband managed to work as farmers, eventually owning four acres of land, animals, and tools. But in 1895 her husband left, their prosperity was declining, and she ultimately lost the farm. It could be that the woman frozen at prayer is a self-portrait, and one of the male figures, a portrait of her husband.

Frame twelve is a recurrence of the sort of natural event pictured in frame eight. The red light night of 1846, as Marie Jeane Adams states, was another meteor shower — the month of August was noted for such events that year. The frame is colored red — Shàngó's color.

Frame thirteen, as Marie Jeane Adams has said, and as I have written elsewhere (Cliff, 1982), is the square in the quilt which most directly addresses the situation of Black people in slavery and the consequences for the whites who enslaved them, as Mrs. Powers envisions these conditions and consequences. The frame contains the largest single figure on the quilt, the hog Betts, and is accompanied by the longest written description.

Frame thirteen shows the figures of a son and daughter of Virginia slaveholders; in their attitudes and shapes they are mirror images of the figures of Adam and Eve in the fourth frame. Here the image of Mawu-Lisa is reversed — the moon is above the male figure; the sun is above the female figure. Their arms, like the arms of Adam and Eve, are upraised; but they are not clasped because a clock separates them. The clock represents the source of their sin — their arrogance in wanting to stop time — which has condemned them to "everlasting punishment." This desire to stop time may be meant by Mrs. Powers as a reference to the former slaveholders who wished for a return to slavery, and their desire to suspend the natural historical movement of Black people from emancipation to full citizenship.

Beneath the two human figures is the hog Betts, a female figure, described by Powers as "independent," who ran 500 miles from Georgia to Virginia. As I said above, the textile designers of Dahomey commonly used animal figures to symbolize African kings in their wall hangings. I take Betts as such a symbolic representation — a metaphor of a Black woman; and her 500 — mile flight is meant to inform us that she was a runaway slave. And that Betts became free on her own account.

Bob Johnson and Kate Bell, with their arrogance and in their punishment, the clock separating the two figures like the tree and entwined serpent in classical representations of the fall of Adam and Eve, stand for another fall from God's grace. The fall earned by whites who enslaved Africans and justified their political and social system. Some wanting to maintain the system, even if it meant stopping the clock.

The penultimate frame continues the creation of the animals.

The final frame is Mrs. Powers's representation of the crucifixion of

Christ, another Biblical assurance of the ultimate redemption of men and women by God, an echo of the first frame in the quilt. The Roman crosses of the crucifixion, as the Kongo crosses which are motifs in the frame depicting the story of Job, promising a continuity of life for the righteous, and a deliverance from the powers of the *beast* of Revelation. In one sense it is a hopeful ending to the journey represented by the Second Bible Quilt; in another sense it is dismal, suggesting that only the death of the Son of God can redeem the casualties of the slavocracy.

IV

> When I plant my garden, I like to plant potatoes when the nights are dark, when the moon is old. and I like to plant my beans when the sign is in the Twins, that's in the arms. You plant your potatoes when the sign is in the feet. Plant cabbage when the sign's in the head, when it's light.
> — Viola King Barnett

Viola King Barnett is one of the older Black women of North Carolina whose histories and testimonies make up the book *Hope and Dignity* (1983): with very few exceptions among these women, one thing is clear, the expectation of a private relationship with God which takes precedence above all other relationships.

It is a truism in American culture and society that older Black women have been among the most supportive of church, consistent voices in the maintenance of the discipline and ethics taught by the church, extraordinary advocates of tolerance and patience. But this is not at all the whole truth.

I see Viola King Barnett alone in her garden, constructing, organizing her plantings, designing her rows according to the signs in the heavens. Like an African gardener.

I see a line of descent from other Black women to Mrs. Barnett. A line in which African belief systems coexist with Afro-American Christianity.

As I mentioned above, it has struck me again and again while working on this essay, that the power assumed and given older women in Africa was substantial — particularly power to do with the spiritual and with life and death. Nana Bukúu — "a superlative warrior, utterly fearless." Yemoja — an "arbiter of her people's happiness and a militant witch." Oshun — "She greets the most important matter in the water." The composers of the funeral and death songs. The dancers of the womb dance.

This female authority came with African men and women to the New World and the slave communities. In the content of their minds and memories. It was embodied in Grandy Nanny. Harriet Tubman. Sojourner Truth. Big Lucy. Mammy Pleasant. Harriet Powers.

The contemporary Black artist, now in her nineties, Minnie Evans has said:

> Art is a mystery ... It's a great mystery. So many dreams have come to me. Big birds flying in the air and a lot of people was dropping bombs in the street, and they was saying, "War, war." A big crowd in the street ... The world is filled with darkness ... So many gods, so many creeds, so many paths that wind and wind. *While just the art of being kind is all the sad world needs. That's right. All the sad world needs.* (my emphasis) (Wilson ed. 1983: 40).

When discussing, examining, analyzing any part of Afro-American history or culture it is necessary always to keep in mind the fact that racism is a primary reality; it is racism that creates the conditions under which Afro-Americans do anything in American culture. It is like trying to work and live and create in an astrodome — an enormous astrodome whose roof can block the sun. Racism creates an unnatural atmosphere, as does the closed-circuit air supply of the astrodome. It is always there. Sometimes not as visible as other times — but everpresent. The atmosphere in the astrodome may seem to change, to freshen, but that is basically an illusion, controlled by those who control the opening and closing of the dome.

Because of segregation — one manifestation of racism in America — African culture was able to survive in some form among Black Americans. Unlike other Americans, who were unable to assimilate to some extent into the dominant culture, Afro-Americans have not for the most part had assimilation as an option. So Africanism survives, and it gives strength and depth to Black life. But because of racism, some of the truly *wonderful* aspects of African philosophy will never enter the mainstream of America and that may be, the American tragedy.

NOTES

1) The title of this essay comes from Ntozake Shange's choreopoem *for colored girls who have considered suicide/ when the rainbow is enuf*. The statement, spoken at the end of the play by the women whose stories we have just heard, is startling. It is an African statement, an affirmation of the divinity of the Black women, of all life.

2) A brief summary of the activities of these people should suffice: Frederick Douglass, was a former slave who became a Black activist and leader of the Abolitionist movement: Sojourner Truth, a former slave, was a feminist as well as a Black leader; Harriet Tubman was a leader of the underground railroad; W.E.B. DuBois, black philosopher and educator, also a Marxist, was a founder of the Harlem Renaissance; Lorraine Hansberry was a Black Civil Rights activist, writer, play-wright, author of *A Raisin in the Sun*. DuBois wrote *The Souls of Black Folk,* 1903.

3) Mammy Pleasant was a Black freewoman who owned property in San Fransisco and lived there. John Brown has a white, a militant opponent of slavery. In 1859 he led a raid on the military arsenal at Harper's Ferry, Virginia, but he was caught, and executed shortly thereafter. His troops were either killed in the raid or executed afterwards; they included Black and white men. In planning the raid, Brown was assisted by advice from Harriet Tubman and money from Mammy Pleasant.

4) Despite her activity as a spy for the Union army, and her role as a leader of her people — or perhaps because of the latter — Harriet Tubman was denied a federal pension even though numerous petitions were made on her account. Following Billie Holiday's adoption of "Strange Fruit" as somewhat of a signature tune, she was arrested and imprisoned for heroin possession; as a result she lost her cabaret license, which was never reinstated. Nina Simone has been charged by the IRS to the tune (no pun intended) of $100.000.

REFERENCES

Adams, Marie Jeanne. 1979. "The Harriet Powers Pictorial Quilts". *Black Art*: 3:4. 12-38.

Bradford, Sarah. 1974. *Harriet Tubman, The Moses of Her People.* rpt. Syracuse: Citadel Press, 118-119.

Cliff, Michelle. 1982. "Object into Subject: Some Thoughts on the Work of Black Women Artists". *Heresies* 15: 34-40; Special Number on *Racism Is the Issue*.

Darden, Norma Jean and Carole. 1978. *Spoonbread and Strawberry Wine*. New York: Fawcett Press.

Hare, Maud Cuney. 1967. "The Source". In *The Negro in Music and Art*. International Library of Negro Life and History.

Hurston, Zora Neale. 1938. *Tell My Horse*. Philadelphia: Lippincott.

-----. 1939. *Moses, Man of the Mountain*. Philadelphia: Lippincott.

Jackson, Irene V. 1981. "Black Women and Music: A Survey from Africa to the New World". In *The Black Woman Cross-Culturally*. Filomena Chioma Steady (ed.), Cambridge: Schenkman, 383-384.

James, C.L.R. 1980. "The Atlantic Slave Trade". In *The Future in the Present: Selected Writings*. Westport: Lawrence Hill & Co.

Thompson, Robert Farris. 1983. *Flash of the Spirit*. New York: Random

House.

Wilson, Emily Herring. 1983. *Hope and Dignity: Older Black Women of the South*, photographs by Susan Mullaly. Philadelphia: Temple University Press.

Concluding Remarks

In summing up the outcome of the essays, I am particularly struck by the "who is *we*?" purposely asked by Adrienne Rich — thus making of simple ordinary pronouns a political statement — in the penetrating and thought provoking keynote address which inaugurates this volume. I would like to reflect further on how political pronouns can be. To become aware of the plural — *we* — a pronoun of power and solidarity (called such by Brown, Gilman 1960), is also to realize the range of two opposing forces: the solidarity or the estrangement this pronoun can create. The pronoun uncovers to all, many questions on the objective relationship existing between speaker and addressee: it concerns not knowing who is the *we* or having difficulty in saying *we* and finally, as Rich concludes from her location, as an American, white, feminist; the *we* who are not the same, the many who do not want to be the same. Within this scope, the *we* can also be uttered, I infer, in complicity with racist and ethnocentric prejudices; therefore, much must be known and shared so as not to use the traditional version of the plural collective stripped of its power. Pronouns give away ideological, social and political views which must be taken into account seriously. *We*, as the Webster *Dictionary* defines it, is the nominative case of the personal pronoun, *us* the objective, *our* and *ours* the possesive, and *ourselves* the intensive and reflexive. *We/us, our/ours — ourselves* — , weakened and neutralized by norms, uses and customs. Yet if one could delete the whole *we* one would leave a much smaller and much inferior world.

Let us not dismiss easily the problem such pronouns present, and elaborate further basing our analysing on recent work on linguistics. In a situation of utterance, there is a reality behind and 'I' and a 'you': 'I' means the speaker who makes the utterance in the moment of discourse, which contains the 'I' and is addressed to as a 'you' (Benveniste 1966: I, 173). But the *I/we* are the subjects of performative utterances; as J.L. Austin clearly stated "there must exist an accepted conventional procedure having a certain effect, that procedure to include the uttering of certain words by certain persons in certain circumstances; and [...] the particular persons and circumstances in a given case must be appropriate for the invocation of the particular procedure invoked" (1978: 27). Furthermore (and the statement is relevant to our point), Austin adds, that the *I/we* who is doing the action "does come essentially to the picture; an advantage because the feature of the speech situation is made explicit" (p. 61). Thus, we must agree that the interesting thing about such pronouns is their "close association with two dimensions fundamental to the analysis of all social life — the dimensions of power and solidarity" (fully developed by Brown, Gilman 253). There is, then, an intimate connection between social structure and group ideology and the use of pronouns.

Evidently then, pronoun usage reflect power relations; basic questions, which I will describe thus arise. Are these 'I/you' allies, are they enemies? The *we* Rich implies in her essay is the common suffering, rather than the common happiness and it is inferred that the 'we' has to discover from where the emptiness of this pronoun rightly comes. One should start with a basic assumption. There is, a *we* — life that surfaces more and more clearly as the muted or silenced voices (using Ch. Kramarae's 1981 pertinent concept), that regains its strength of utterance. No fact is too little to let it slip through our fingers and besides the interest in facts themselves, there is that power 'we' may acquire by changing facts and transforming history.

Who is *we*? Three areas of research clearly emerge from the questions the six articles in this volume bring to light, which can be broadly integrated to the semiotics of culture; the diversities in which sex oppression is made manifest according to cultural, class and ethnic divergences. Let me underline that these articles — although different in scope — by and large present specific aspects of the semiotics of culture (employing Díaz-Diocaretz's theoretical framework). Particular importance has been attached to the questions of hierarchical structure of the languages of culture. These papers point to the divergence and complexity involved in the making of hierarchies, toward demonstrating — to quote the Russian semiotician Yuri Lotman (1975) — that "the concept of culture is inseparably linked with the opposition of its 'non-culture'" (p. 57). Within this framework, they show the dialectic relationship between culture and its outer-sphere. The oppositions suggested are created by the active role of the outer-space in the mechanisms of culture. The paradigms of extra-cultural spaces *we* (all of us) are given, in whose center a certain normal 'we' is situated, to which other people are opposed as a paradigmatic set of anomalies (p. 60). Taking Lotman as a point of departure, I propose that this 'we' and that 'you' can be topics of inquiry in their antithetical opposition: enlightenment/ignorance, belonging to an ethnic group/ not belonging to it, European/non-European, male/female, culture/

non-culture, central/peripheral. These meaningful oppositions are ideological and they can be broadened — part/whole; member/segment; bound/free. The foundation of these ideological oppositions, as social formations are founded on a double armature — patriarchy as an oppressor/enslaver and the ethico-political superstructures constituted by systems of value and mental representations which try to determine what is central and marginal or peripheral. These, I believe, are the opposing forces the essays explore, re-claiming history, art, language.

One such way of illustrating this point will reveal an interesting vein of oppositions: the dictionary can be an enlightening source of information. The barring of certain connotations seems to be more than a matter of usage. I look up the word *colonization* (so widely used in this volume) in the Webster and the entry reads:

> the act of colonizing, or state of being colonized [...] *Colonization society*; formerly a society in the United States designed to aid free Negroes in emigrating to Africa.

For the same reason *colonialism* is thus:

> (1) a phrase, idiom, practice, etc. peculiar to a colony (2) the colonial policy or system of extending territory.

Peculiar to colonial policy; yes, indeed, but forced by *whom*? The 'I' and 'you' implicit in such system have been falsified and the dictionary reveals a neutralized description of the arsenal of facts some *we* must recuperate. Anybody looking carefully at dictionaries will realize that the descriptive set of some definitions consistently support a whole doctrine. This aseptic entry is subject to change if people want to make their interest engage and pursue a common task. The colonial system means — in reality (as can be inferred from the papers of Cliff, Díaz-Diocaretz, Essed) — direct capitalist exploitation, without military occupation (neo-colonialism), in Karl Marx's more realistic definition in the *Capital*. A more recent one, which takes into account both economic and ethnic considerations is as follows: "the point of reference is a government by people of one culture over people of a different culture — usually of Europeans over non-Europeans." In short, "domination by people of another culture", which is equally possible within an independent state, in Philip D. Curtin's sensible discussion (1974: 22-23). These definitions should not obscure the fact that the colonial relationship chained the colonizer and the colonized into an implacable dependence, molded their respective characters and dictated their conduct (on this interaction see A. Memmi

1965). Because of social and intellectual subordination one class (race) borrows a world view from another class and asserts this borrowed world view in words, in A. Gramsci's lucid analysis (1948). Or, in the well chosen metaphorical reality of Martinican Franz Fanon, "Black Skin, white masks". The quotation I would like to close with, is Aimé Césaire's: colonization is not evangelization, nor philantropic enterprise, nor a desire to push back ignorance, nor an attempt to extend law. The decisive actors — in the Martinican's strong description — are the adventurer and the pirate, the grocer and the shipowner, the gold digger and the merchant, appetite and force and

> a form of civilization which [...] finds itself obliged [...] to extend to a world scale the competition of its antagonistic economies. (1950, in 1972)

The distinctions themselves are basic; to be aware of these distinctions is a theorethical weapon to 'draw a dividing line' between true and false ideas (paraphrasing Lenin's words). A question I want to bring for consideration is implicit in these six essays: how words are exploited by one or more ideologies which in turn use them to fight and kill other true words vital to those who make history. The philosophical fight over words — pronouns in our case — is a part of a political fight that *we* experience every day; an essentially defensive not an offensive struggle. And the fight over words should not be underestimated — as performative utterances, words mean whatever the powers or institutions want to mean (Medina's examples on legal definitions are illuminating).

Let us return to the dictionary, clearly an instrument of the ideologies and institutions in power, which records the authoritative word and silences — or else gives a negative recording — of those vital words which are the *abcd* of consciousness and self-knowledge. We must agree on one basic presupposition: that indeed colonialism is a policy or system of extending territory. No more than that. Facts are overwhelming as to the thefts and massacres that paved the way to colonialism (and imperialism) into human history. It is even more apparent according to the data M. Cliff provides: millions were forced to the Americas from the various domains of different African cultures. In just one area of the world, as the anthropologist S. Mintz affirms, "no one who was not European ever migrated to the Caribbean region freely" (1974: 47). The vitality of this forced labor in contemporary societies as active agents of opposing cultures and ideologies is an important area of research.

It appears then, that we are to aim at proverbial simplicity. Let us return to the opening question of my remarks — who is the *we*? Who is the "We the people" which heads most constitutions in the world? Let us also try to identify who is the *we/our* implied in many political statements as pronouns of solidarity. One such, which comes to mind, is a document sent to a newspaper in Cuba in 1928 on the founding of the Ku Klux Klan: the Order — the document reads — is oriented towards "the defense and conservation of the motherland Cuba, its Constitution and Laws." The most obvious question is, whose motherland are the signatories — an American and a Cuban — talking about, or whose Cuba? Evidently not that of those who did not migrate to the Caribbean region freely, nor to their descendants. Examples of these falsified solidarity invocations abound, and they are part of a huge corpus to be deconstructed. No misreading is possible.

The pronoun of solidarity is, as I have argued, a very complex phenomenon, and it gives away ideological and political views. There is the *we* uttered to marginalize, alienate, repress a 'you' (*them*, *they*), but there is also the *we* of the culturally, socially and ethnically oppressed, as these essays suggest, who refuse to be centralized and speak from the periphery asserting their difference. Insofar as ethnic or culturally different groups, the accounts collected by demographers as to mass suicides, ruin, weariness, death (perpetual death) with which the colonized peoples reacted to the "colonial policy or system of extending territory" — in the neat, asceptic entry of the Webster's *Dictionary*. However, the essays in this volume, which analyse black culture in the United States, show that even a brutal slave regime, reinforced by racist ideology, could not crush the human spirit. The words of the Russian poet Osip Mandelstam can be extrapolated for our purpose, and they deserve close attention:

> Just as there are two geometries [...] there are two histories [...], written in different keys: one that speaks only of acquisitions, another only of losses, and both would be speaking of one and the same thing. (1977: 67)

A clarifying statement should be made on the concept of *race* used in this volume, as the oppostion of pertaining or not to a given ethnic group (mainly the opposition white-European/non-European). Claude Lévy-Strauss made it easily understood in *Race et histoire* (1952); modern genetic studies deny a purely biological notion of race; in any case, no psychological feature can be ascribed to any race, and on top of it all, the threatening principle of race (racism) is that it presupposes inferiorities and superiorities, and not simple divergences. In fact, as French historian Pierre Vilar lucidly sums it up (1980: 152-153): *racism* is but an aspect of the instinctive contempt certain groups feel towards others who are in the exterior circumference of their group. Racism and xenophobia — Vilar asserts — are birds of a feather. The world is not divided in races, but in multiplicity of *cultures*; in complex combination. Racial problems are strongly linked to social classes (social hierarchization and social and economic exploitation). While racism is understood in terms of its economic and political functions, ethnocentrism constitutes how people of any group look down on those who score poorly against the values around which the first group is built.

Let us bring other problems into closer focus, other aspects of ordinary language. What are some of the rights the *we* — women, colonized (through racism, ethnocentrism) have been denied? The door opens and light and fresh air come in: the denial (if we agree on the implied theoretical framework of these papers), is the whole performative utterance of the simple ordinary pronouns — *I/you*; *we/they*; *us*, *ourselves*. And so much needs to be done — these essays suggest — in real, everyday life, to identify tools of oppression (Essed's research within the midst of one of the more liberal societies in Europe is a step ahead). Therefore, for third world (which is more all inclusive), a full identification of the language (performative acts) of the oppressor is imperative; quantitative research on this direction should be pursued further to make the whole map visible. To identify expressions of subordination or of the non-reciprocal power pronoun takes us also to legal discriminatory language, such as the one C. Medina has uncoverd for some Latin American countries. Laws may be mere conventions, but habits and customs make them a convenience devised for the support of natures not allowed to lay down laws themselves. It is not difficult to see what power the *we* is to invoke, without muffling opinions and speaking out-right; to make it a performative utterance, and not to be lead by the nose, by authority — *ipse dixit*.

And on we go; to begin with, the *we* has not been lead by the nose — memory mechanisms (of oral tradition) pervade up to the XXth century (see Cliff, Díaz-Diocaretz). And since the colonized did not freely give in, what more natural, then, than to analyze the formidable obstacles they were trying to tamper with incorruptible conscience? And that is, no more nor less, than history, than culture itself. The known facts show that only certain gratitudes and hostilities inspire us; that certain paths lead to fertile land. Feminist studies — within this perspective — suggest that perhaps it may be worth while to attempt some account. Naturally, no single word reaches the center of three targets.

There remain other aspects to be unveiled — if art is/were to be *mimesis*, there lies all that corpus of visual and written discourses where the female body (the 'other') is muted, used; an object of desire and disgust. The female body, used in mass media, communication, food pornography — as R. Coward strongly points out. The female body, it should be stressed, is used in Western and Westernized cultures as a commodity, regardless of ethnic and/or cultural differentiations. Studies in this direction would reveal fruitful areas of analysis. The sexual self-discovery of women has not changed men nor their privileges (Coward asserts); female desire and female sexuality are still governed by achieving ideals imposed by the patriarchal world. To deconstruct these codes, symbols and emblems imposed by media would surely provoke a shattering transformation. More research into this area should be developed to show — if any — the different cultural and/or moral codes which influence "female desire".

In the last years feminist scholarship has explored the significance of gender and its influence (inception) in other activities: reading experience, woman's writing, status and dependence of women in social, political, economic, cultural structures. Feminist critics have re-evaluated, discovered, celebrated neglected works and investigated the image of women in the works of an author, a genre, a period, as well as feminist poetics and the distinctiveness of women's writing. Work has also been done on history — the role women have played in changing history, their fight in revolutionary struggles, their labor force, their political and social conditions. There has also been renewed attention, more subtle and more sweeping, on crafts, music, oral tradition, general process of language change.

The essays in this volume offer arguments to develop further other considerations of self-identity, self-affirmation and social identitiy, as well as inclusion/exclusion within cultural space, making room for alternatives to develop critical attitudes in which the concepts of male authority (patriachal world) are inscribed within a large social system and a larger authoritative and/or repressive framework. This is where they will have direct and significant political relevance.

Needless to say how feminist scholarship in the last decade has made us attend to the notion of sexuality (important works on textuality and sexuality abound), as well as path-breaking investigation on linguistic, sociological, political, historical problems. The scope of feminist inquiry and its critical debate cannot be underestimated — the huge bibliography about the state of the scholarship on specific issues has been widely described in the last couple of years. There are also abundant anthologies and compilations of essays on historical issues, ethnic considerations, politics of sexuality; these topics have increasingly received attention in a meaningful category of experience. (The wide variety of references and works each contributor to this volume provides, allows me to refrain from enumerating them).

New approaches are sure to come forth: a 1980 perspective, like the one suggested in this volume, neatly presents three structures in a complex unity: sex, race, class. As a *we* who is both the same and dissimilar, situations vary. Whereas the patriarchal world de-territorializes women in general (to use Díaz-Diocaretz's clarifying notion 1984), ethnic minorities are forced to make particular adaptations to the social system (and no simple explanation of them can be accepted), forced by threatening ethnocentric principles. Within this de-territorialized frontier, blacks, *latinas*, American indians (from the North and the South of the borders) and third world are double minorities — minorities within minorities, with double oppressions and double bondages to free from the rights and prejudices which 'legally' inabilitate women within societies. Research in this area will provide the opportunity for the survival of many and strengthen women's role as independent figures within societies and cultures of that nature. The relevant features of re-territorialization of culture in its diversity is surely an important step forward.

Some other points of reflection which these articles suggest to me spring from other areas of knowledge. The debate which has revolved around whether or not American blacks (and for that matter any oppressed minority) possess a distinct cultural heritage and its subversive element and transgressions are amply documented in this volume. These excluded double minorities (of which black are here the best represented) demand re-examination in other colonial (or colonized) societies. The impressive movement of population and cultures, woman labor and struggle should be further traced. One must surely account for their denial, rejection and disassociation from the dominant culture (class, race), in trying to reach an understanding of the structure and forcefulness of ethnocentric-sexual attitudes. As the papers here suggest, these attitudes should not and cannot be studied for their content alone, but to evaluate their force and extension as well, in their diverse historical experiences of different classes — the various stages of female consciousness within their social, racial and class *milieu* need to be considered in the future. Recent literature is moving toward these directions.

What becomes clear in this theoretical framework, are the diversities of oppression according to class, race and even geographical location; although male authority pervades thus imposing sexual differences, feminist studies must surely accept the differences (same/dissimilar) and not impose a fictitious homogeneity. Although there are common struggles, other sectors of the same gender collective may (and most surely do) have different priorities. Also, within a same social system, the struggles and objectives of its outer-space cultural and ethnic components will necessarily be centered on different targets. The 'we' then regains its true essence (existence, reality) of plurality instead of covering (veiling) a majestic 'we' which stands for authoritative discourse of the 'normal we'. That false *we* through which the *pax romana* has been imposed; the *we* which represents that the speaker is the summation of the people and can speak as their representative; *we* can be a pronoun of estrangement. Plurality is an old ubiquitous metaphor for power (on this see Brown, Gilman 1960).

To sum up the arguments raised in these essays. The most elementary remark upon present feminist studies can hardly avoid these considerations, and some mention that there exists more than one sort of oppression (sexual) upon women throughout the earth, nor can it avoid the role of women in anti-imperialist struggle. These issues promise continuing controversy. Historical testimonies abound and should be seized and used as the arsenal of experiences to be recoded in *memory*, as a key to understanding the present. While women share many features based on broad and common historical and sexual experiences, each class, race, location is in its own way particular and distinctive. Models and preconceptions cannot be transferred uncritically. Though these problems cannot receive here the full treatment they deserve, there are useful perspectives upon the field of women's studies and feminist identity. Some of the aspects discussed in these six essays, are the areas which will probably undergo serious revision when the nature of *difference* is fully understood. The politics then, seems to be to de-colonize and de-matriarchize (which in reality means de-Westernize) feminist studies, drawing the boundaries; the challenge is clear as to what our role and preoccupations ought to be. Going back to Adrienne Rich's challenging question of who is the *we*, which introduced an important dimension I have tried to pursue; what these essays are saying then amounts to a *simple* fact — 'we' cannot say 'we' with *simple* conviction; it is a common suffering and also the effort and desire for a common happiness that produces the sense of community that can be shared in order to realize a *simple* truth: "You cannot speak for me. I cannot speak for you."

Iris M. Zavala
Amsterdam, 1984

REFERENCES

Austin, J.L. 1978. *How to do Things with Words* (1962). Cambridge: Harvard Univ. Press.

Benveniste, Emile. 1966. *Problèmes de linguistique générale*. Paris: Gallimard, I.

Brown, Roger and Albert Gilman. 1960. "The Pronouns of Power and Solidarity". In Thomas A. Sebeok (ed). *Style in Language*. Mass: MIT Press: 253-276.

Césaire, Aimé. 1972. *Discourse on Colonialism (1950)*. New York: Monthly Review Press.

Curtin Philip D. 1974. "The Black Experience of Colonialism and Imperialism". *Daedalus*. Special Issue: *Slavery, Colonialism and Racism*: 17-30.

Díaz-Diocaretz, Myriam. 1984. *The Transforming Power of Language. The Poetry of Adrienne Rich*. Utrecht: HES Publisher.

Gramsci, Antonio. 1948. *Il materialismo storico e la filosofia di Benedetto Croce*. Roma: Einaudi.

Kramarae, Cheris. 1981. *Women and Men Speaking*. Mass.: Newbury House Publishers.

Lotman, Yuri *et al.* 1975. "Theses on the Semiotic Study of cultures (As Applied to Slavic Texts). In Thomas A. Sebeok (ed). *The Tell-Tale Sign: A Survey of Semiotics*. Lisse/Netherlands: The Peter de Ridder: 57-83.

Mandelstam, Osip. 1977. "About the Nature of the Word". *Selected Essays*, tr. Sidney Monas. Austin: TX: 67.

Memmi, A. 1965. *The Colonizer and the Colonized*. In Stanley J. Stein and Barbara H. Stein. 1970. *The Colonial Heritage of Latin America. Essays on Economic Dependence in Perspective*. New York: Oxford Univ. Press.

Vilar, Pierre. 1980. *Iniciación al vocabulario del análisis histórico*. Barcelona: Crítica.

Contributors Notes

MICHELLE CLIFF is a Jamaican writer. Her published work includes *Claiming an Identity they Taught me to Despise* (1980) and the novel *Abeng* (1983); forthcoming in fall 1985 is a volume of prose and poetry entitled *The Land of Look Behind*. She has lectured widely in the United States and published in many feminist journals and magazines; she is in the editorial board of *Signs*.

ROSALIND COWARD, British, lectures in Media Studies at Reading University. An active feminist since the seventies, she has published three books: *Language and Materialism. Developments in Semiology and the Theory of the Subject*, with John Ellis (1977), *Patriarchal Precedents* (1983) and *Female Desire* (1984), as well as articles in *M/F*, *Feminist Review*, *Screen*, *Spare Rib*, *The Guardian*.

MYRIAM DÍAZ-DIOCARETZ, Chilean poet and translator who now lives in Holland. Has done work on translation studies, American literature, Black American Women Poets, as well as translations of American poetry. She has published articles in the United States, Europe and Latin America. Her published work includes *The Transforming Power of Language. The Poetry of Adrienne Rich* (1984); forthcoming is an anthology of Rich's poetry into Spanish and the book *Translating Poetic Discourse: Questions on Strategies on Adrienne Rich*. She is researcher of the Faculty of Letters, University of Utrecht and now Visiting Scholar in Residence, University of Mississippi.

PHILOMENA ESSED is a Surinamese and lives in The Netherlands. Has an MA in Social Anthropology from the University of Amsterdam, and has published "Racisme en feminisme" (Racism and Feminism) and *Alledaags Racisme* (*Everyday Racism* 1984), a book based in fieldwork in Holland and in the United States. She is guest lecturer in Ethnic Studies at the University of Amsterdam.

CECILIA MEDINA is a Chilean lawyer who now resides in Holland. She is a researcher at the Europa Instituut in Utrecht and is finishing her doctor's degree on law in Civil Rights. She has worked on civil rights in the United States and Europe.

ADRIENNE RICH is the author of twelve books of poems and two of prose. She has taught writing and women's studies at universities throughout the United States, and has read her poetry and lectured at colleges, universities, women's centers and conferences in North America, France, The Netherlands, Italy, Great Britain and Japan. Her poetry and prose have been translated into Dutch, German, Spanish, French, Italian, Swedish and Japanese. Since the early 1970's her life and work have been shaped by her commitment to the women's liberation movement. She has been active in feminist struggles against racism and anti-Semitism, for lesbian rights, and in the lesbian and feminist press and periodical network.

IRIS M. ZAVALA, born in Puerto Rico, is the author of more than fourteen books of literary criticism, history of ideas and political history of Spain and Latin America. She has published four books of poetry, a novel *Kiliagonía* (*Chiliagony*), just translated into English, and a second novel, *Nocturna más no funesta* (*Nocturne but not mournful*) is in press. Her work has been translated into English, French, Portuguese, Greek, Dutch. She now lives in Amsterdam and is presently Chair of Hispanic Literatures in the University of Utrecht.

In the CRITICAL THEORY series the following titles have been published:

1. DÍAZ-DIOCARETZ, Myriam and Iris M. ZAVALA (eds.): *WOMEN, FEMINIST IDENTITY AND SOCIETY IN THE 1980's. Selected Papers.* Amsterdam, 1985.
2. DÍAZ-DIOCARETZ, Myriam: *Translating Poetic Discourse: Questions of Feminist Strategies in Adrienne Rich.* Amsterdam, 1985.
3. DIJK, Teun A. van (ed.): *DISCOURSE AND LITERATURE. New Approaches to the Analysis of Literary Genres.* Amsterdam, 1985.

ADH-1514

WITHDRAWN
From Bertrand Library

DATE DUE

DEC 1 3 1996